CHURCHES of ISTANBUL

Uranus Photography Agency Publishing Co.

URANUS

CHURCHES of İSTANBUL

URANUS PHOTOGRAPHY AGENCY PUBLISHING CO.

Publisher:
Uranus Photography Agency Publishing Co.
Ankara Caddesi, Cağaloğlu Yokuşu, No:33,
Evren Han Kat:2/40,
Eminönü, Istanbul-Turkey
Phone: +90 212 5280158
www.uranus.com.tr
info@uranus.com.tr

Editor:
Nurhayat Yazıcı

Text:
Ali Kılıçkaya

Photographs:
Erdal Yazıcı
www.erdalyazici.com

Art Direction:
Haluk Celkan

Cover & Book Design
Alşimist VCA - Haluk Celkan
www.alsimist.com

Maps
Desen Atölyesi -Olgun Üstün
Alşimist VCA

English Translation:
Batı Tercüme Dil Hizmetleri

English Proofreading:
Steve O'Farrell

Printing / Colour Separation:
Acar Group Printing Industry and
Commercial Investments JSC
Phone: +90 212 4221800

ISBN: 978-605-5940-01-0

1st edition: April 2008

CONTENT

Chapter I

HISTORIC PENINSULA and FORTRESS INTERIOR

Chapter II

CHURCHES OF THE GOLDEN HORN

Chapter III

CHURCHES OF BEYOĞLU / ŞiŞLi

Chapter IV

CHURCHES OF BOSPHORUS - KADIKÖY - ISLANDS

NORTH AMERICA
EUROPA
TÜRKİYE
ASIA
PASIFIC OCEAN
NORTH ATLANTIC OCEAN
PASIFIC OCEAN
AFRICA
SOUTH AMERICA
SOUTH ATLANTIC OCEAN
INDIAN OCEAN
AUSTRALIA
TÜRKİYE in the WORLD
İSTANBUL in the TÜRKİYE
BLACK SEA
ANKARA
AEGEAN SEA
MEDITERRANEAN SEA
BELGRAD ORM
dolmabahçe palace
dolmabahçe clock tower
EUROPEAN SIDE
galata tower
saint antoine church
GAZİOSMANPAŞA
kariye museum
EYÜP
BAĞCILAR
GÜNEŞLİ
EDİRNEKAPI
zeyrek mosque
TOPKAPI
AKSARAY
ŞİRİNEVLER
ZEYTİNBURNU
YEDİKULE
ATATÜRK HAVALİMANI (AIRPORT)
BAKIRKÖY
süleymaniye mosque
FLORYA
YEŞİLKÖY
sultanahmet mosque
hagia sophia
hagia eirene

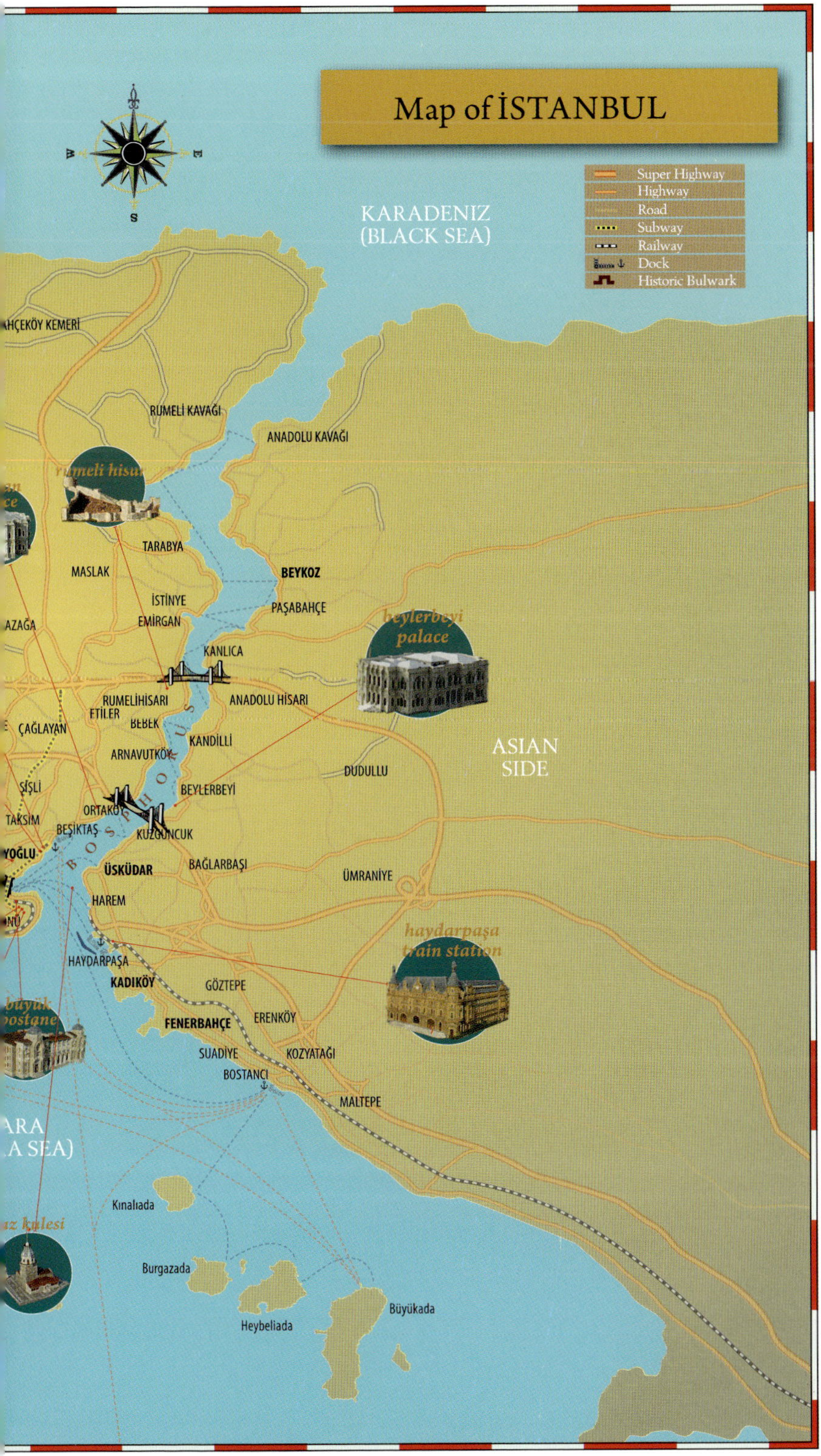
Map of İSTANBUL
Super Highway
Highway
Road
Subway
Railway
Dock
Historic Bulwark
KARADENIZ
(BLACK SEA)
RUMELİ KAVAĞI
ANADOLU KAVAĞI
rumeli hisar
TARABYA
MASLAK
BEYKOZ
İSTİNYE
EMİRGAN
PAŞABAHÇE
beylerbeyi palace
KANLICA
RUMELİHİSARI
ETİLER
ANADOLU HİSARI
BEBEK
ÇAĞLAYAN
KANDİLLİ
ARNAVUTKÖY
ASIAN SIDE
DUDULLU
ŞİŞLİ
BEYLERBEYİ
ORTAKÖY
TAKSİM
BEŞİKTAŞ
KUZGUNCUK
BOSPHORUS
ÜSKÜDAR
BAĞLARBAŞI
ÜMRANİYE
HAREM
haydarpaşa train station
HAYDARPAŞA
KADIKÖY
GÖZTEPE
ERENKÖY
FENERBAHÇE
SUADİYE
KOZYATAĞI
BOSTANCI
MALTEPE
Kınalıada
Burgazada
Büyükada
Heybeliada

Η ΑΝΑϹΤΑϹΙϹ
ΙϹ
ΧϹ

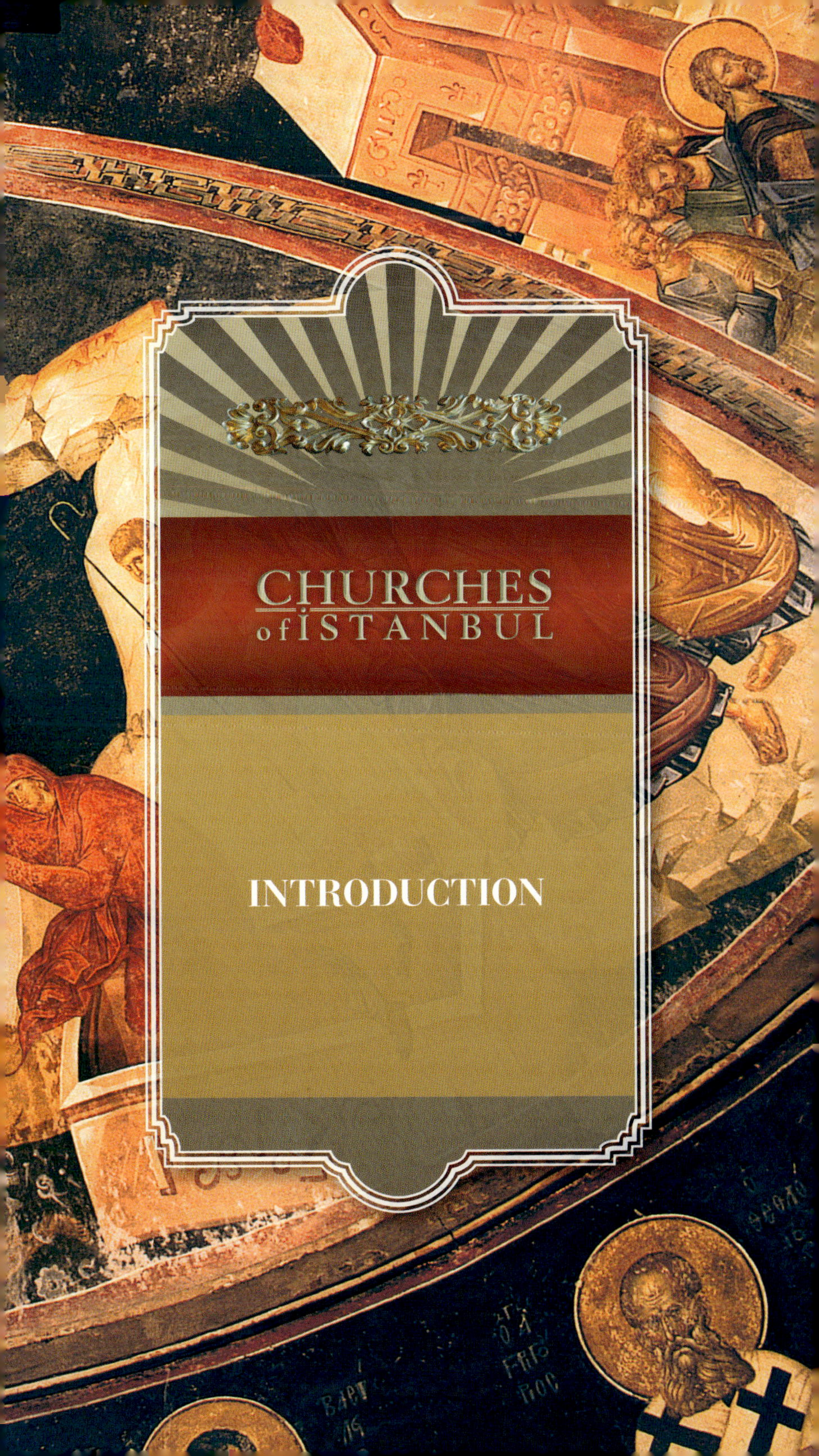

INTRODUCTION

INTRODUCTION

The church is the temple of followers of Christianity, which is one of the three major celestial religions. It is derived from the word "ekklesia", meaning community in Greek. However, in Latin, it comes from the word "ecclesia", meaning the meeting of believers or the place where believers gather.

Christianity was born within the territories of the Roman Empire in the 1st Century CE as a reform of, and a cult of Judaism, and is a religion founded by Jesus of Nazareth, a Jew. The people of this religion had undergone considerable torture, distress and loss of life due to their faith during 300 years in the polytheic Roman Empire. Having become freely practised during the reign of Roman Emperor Constantine I (306-337), the construction of churches as places of Christian worship was commenced. The first of these were called basilicas, in compliance with the concept of religion. Not only businessmen, but also judgement committees would gather there. The name basilica comes from the fact that this judgement committee represented the authority of the emperor, that is to say the "basileus" (king, sovereign).

Basilica, "basilike" in Greek, is the name of the Salon of the Palace where the emperors executed justice. The basilica in Latin means "Court of Justice". Because these Courts of Justice were large and convenient to the cult members most of the time, they were converted into churches by Christians.

The first churches were built in basilical plan. We see that central planned, vaulted, and narthexed churches were constructed in the course of time and later we see the construction of the Greek cross-planned churches. During subsequent centuries we also see the occurrence of churches that show different types, plans, and architectural characteristics. We see that Roman style churches were constructed in the 11th Century, Gothic style in the 12th Century, Renaissance style in the 15th Century, Baroque style in the 16th Century, and modern style dating from the 19th Century.

Seven ecumenical council meetings were carried out at different dates in Anatolia in conjunction with the accordance of freedom to the Christian faith. The first of these, at the time of Emperor Constantine, was held in Nicaea (İznik) in the year 325. Constantinople (the city of Istanbul) played host to three council meetings in the years 381, 553, and 680/81. Also, we see that another council meeting was held in Chalcedon/Kadıköy in the year 451. Thus, Istanbul holds an important place in the history of Christianity.

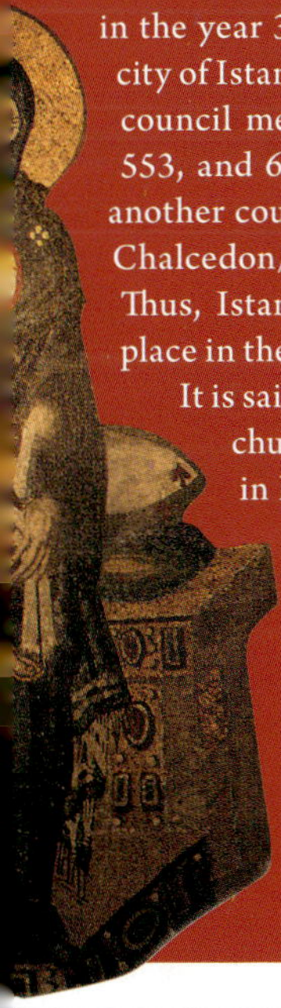

It is said that approximately 500 churches were constructed in Istanbul during the Middle Ages. It has been determined that there were about 50 monasteries and churches at the time of the conquest of Istanbul. After the conquest, these monasteries and churches were converted to large

and small mosques. Some, however, continued to function as churches. The chapels that were not converted to small mosques disappeared as a result of earthquakes, fires, and new construction with the passage of time. Furthermore, the new ones were constructed by sultans' firmans to replace collapsed or damaged churches due to those earthquakes and fires occurring during the Ottoman era. In addition to these churches, others have been renewed in the age of the Turkish Republic.

Today, besides churches belonging to the Protestant, Gregorian and Anglican denominations, most societies of Christian faith in Istanbul belong to the Orthodox and Catholic Churches.

Since discussing and explaining all of the churches that are in contemporary Istanbul would exceed the dimensions of this book, only the more important ones are introduced and discussed here. These include the Church of Pnayia Muhliotissa in Fener which survives to the present day and is still used as a church; the Church of Aya Irini which was converted to a mosque during the Ottoman era; the Church of the Divine Wisdom (church of Hagia Sophia) in Sultanahmet, converted to a mosque in 1453, becoming the Museum of Hagia Sophia in 1935;

the Monastery Church of Khora in Edirne Kapı (Mosque of Kariye in 1511 / Museum of Kariye in 1945); the Church of Sergios and Bakhos in Kadırga (Small Hagia Sophia Mosque); the Pantocrator Monastery Church in Zeyrek (Mosque of Zeyrek); the Church of Ayios Theodoros in Vefa (Church Mosque of Vefa); the Constantine Lips Monastery Church in Aksaray / Vatan Street (Mosque of Fenari İsa); the Monastery Church of Pantepoptes in Fatih (Old Mosque of Alms) and the Monastery Church of Pammakaristos in Fatih (Mosque of Fethiye in 1590, the Parekklesion part of the church became the Museum of Fethiye after 1960); the Church of Aya Teodosia (Mosque of the Rose) in the Golden Horn (Haliç). Other inclusions are some important church structures such as the Church of Saint Antoine and the Church of Santa Maria Draperis in Beyoğlu which were constructed in the Ottoman era and display important architectural characteristics, as well as the Church of Saint Esprit in Harbiye, the Church of Surp Krikor Lusaroviç in Karaköy, the Church of Ayios Constantine-Ayia Eleni in Tarlabaşı, the Church of Surp Asdvadzadzin and the Church of Ayia Kiraki in Kumkapı.

HISTORIC PENINSULA and FORTRESS INTERIOR

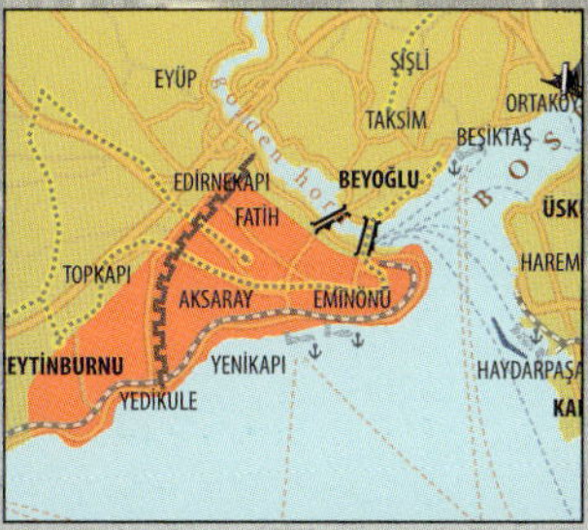

01 HAGIA SOPHIA

Image of Jesus on the panel of the Deisis mosaic

South entrance to the interior narthex

Hagia Sophia, situated in the district of Sultanahmet in Istanbul, is the biggest church constructed in the Byzantine era and has survived intact to the present day. It is one of the masterpieces of architecture in world history. The structure, referred to as Great Church (Megale Ekklesia) when it was first constructed, was dedicated to Divine Wisdom (Holy Sapientia), the second element of the Christian trinity. The current structure is the third Hagia Sophia constructed on the same site and was used first as a church for 916 years, then as a mosque for 481 years, and has been used as a museum since 1935.

The first church, constructed by Emperor Constantine (337-361) in 360, was a basilica with wooden framework. The church was largely burned down in the year 404, during the rebellion that broke out upon the exile of John Chrysostom, Patriarch of Constantinople, who protested the erection of a statue of Eudoxia, wife of the Emperor Arcadius (395-408), in front of Hagia Sophia. The second church, constructed by Emperor Theodosios II (408-450), in place of the original, was opened in the year 415. Some relics belonging to this structure, large marble architectural elements and friezes ornamented with lamb reliefs representing the twelve apostles were revealed after excavation by A.M.Schneider in 1935 and can be seen at the entrance of the current Hagia Sophia.

This church too was burned and collapsed during the rebellion of Nika that broke out in 532 against Emperor Justinian I (527-565). The current Hagia Sophia was constructed between the years 532-537 during the reign of Emperor

Scene from inside Hagia Sophia

Justinian. The architects were Anthemius of Tralles (Aydın) and Isidoros of Miletus (Söke/Balat). The construction of the church was accomplished in a period of five years as a result of the work of thousands of labourers and craftsmen. The materials were brought from ancient cities situated in different regions of the empire and from coloured quarries in Egypt and Teselia. The Temple of Solomon in Jerusalem was renowned as the world's biggest structure at the time; Emperor Iustinianos (Justinian), at a huge inauguration ceremony on December 27th, 537, along with the Patriarch of Constantinople, entered Hagia Sophia via the interior narthex. Confronted with the panorama he gave thanks to God for deeming him

Exterior view of Hagia Sophia

worthy of constructing such a temple and continued, "O Solomon, I have surpassed you!"

When the main dome and the Eastern semi-dome of Hagia Sophia cracked and became dangerous after earthquakes in the years 553 and 557 in Constantinople, restoration commenced immediately. However, the main dome of the church collapsed completely after a third earthquake in 558. At this, Emperor Justinian charged young architect Isidoros, the nephew of Isidoros, one of the original architects of Hagia Sophia, with the church's restoration. He elevated the dome by seven meters and slotted it, using lighter material. The restored church was opened for worship on December 23rd, 562.

View of the southern nave

Hagia Sophia has witnessed many important events throughout history. Emperors were crowned here, victories celebrated, and criminals were given sanctuary. All of the icons were removed from Hagia Sophia during the iconoclastic crisis between the dates of 726-843, at which time antagonism towards icons was prevalent.

Mosaic panel above the Imperial Gate depicting Leo VI kneeling at the feet of Jesus, the Virgin Mary and the Archangel Gabriel.

Hagia Sophia was damaged by fire and earthquake in 859 and 869, and was promptly repaired and reopened for worship. The structure suffered much damage in the great earthquake of 989, when the main dome collapsed. The church was restored in six years by Armenian Architect Tiridat, appointed by Emperor Balileos II (976-1025), and reopened for worship in 994.

Altar of Hagia Sophia

The Latins occupied Constantinople in 1204 during the Fourth Crusade and dominated it until 1261. They plundered Hagia Sophia, transporting holy relics to the West, along with all precious objects. When the city was regained from the Latins in 1261 Hagia Sophia was in a very worn state. Supporting buttresses were added to the North and East parts of the structure during the reign of Emperor Andronicus II (1282-1328). By the time Istanbul was conquered in 1453, Hagia Sophia was in a neglected and ruinous state.

Hagia Sophia is a structure with basilical plan and dome, and consists of two narthexes, interior and exterior, an apse and three naves. Nine doors give entry from the interior narthex to the main floor. The main floor measures 75.5 meters by 69.5 meters excluding the narthexes and apse. At the western end of the northern nave is a marble grade, covered by a bronze plate with a cavity, called "wish stone". In the eastern direction of the middle nave there is an apse. Grade and column arches separating the main floor from the naves are richly ornamented. Monograms invoking the name of the Emperor Justinian are carved on these arches. There is a u-shaped gallery above the interior narthex and lateral naves. One ascends via ramps on the four corners of the structure. The exit of the ramp in the southeast corner is now blocked up by a brick minaret. The western gallery was occupied by the empress, the northern one by the women, and the southern one by the emperor. The door at the southern end of the western gallery leads to the clergymen's rooms. The main dome is slightly elliptical and its diameter ranges from 31 to 32 meters with an elevation of 55 meters, and contains 40 windows on its rim. There are angel portraits on the pendentive of the main dome. There are 107 columns on aggregate, 40 in the lower floor of the structure and 67 of them in the gallery. The floors and walls of the building are covered with white and coloured marble respectively.

Image of the Madonna and Child on the Comnenus mosaic in the South Gallery

There is a square area, bordered by coloured, round-cut stones, on the right frontal side of the main floor. When and for which purpose this place, named Omphalos, was constructed is not clearly understood, although there are some rumours. According to some sources it may have been the location for empirical coronations during the later periods of the Byzantine Empire.

At the northeastern corner of the main building there is an annexed treasury building, known as skevophylakion, which has a cylindrical frame and a dome. Outside the northern door of the interior narthex, on the left hand side, is the baptistery, known as baptisterion.

The mosaics decorating the inside of the structure are largely damaged,

Image of a Saint

View of the northeast gallery

Mosaic in the south gallery depicts Christ flanked by Emperor Constantine IX and his wife, the Empress zone.

have fallen off, or been destroyed by fire, earthquake, and other natural events over the course of history.

These pictorial mosaics, placed in different parts of the building, are significant not only for mosaic art but also for Byzantine history. All of them belong to the post-iconoclastic period (724-843). We can proceed through the mosaics as follows: above the door opening from the interior narthex to the main floor there is a mosaic of Jesus, holding a book in which

Marble urn from Pergamum.

Image of the Archangel Gabriel on the arch of the southern dais in the apse of Hagia Sophia

Images of Emperor John Comnenus II, Madonna and Child, with Empress Irene on the Comnenus mosaic panel in the south gallery.

Mosaic panel above the south door of the interior narthex depicting Constantine I, Madonna and Child, and Justinian I.

Image of Emperor John Comnenus II on the Comnenus mosaic panel

is written, "God bless you", and "I am the light of the world", and, kneeling at his feet, the Emperor Leo VI (886-912). On either side, in round panels, are depicted the Virgin Mary and the Archangel Gabriel. Above the southern entrance of the interior

View from the gallery

Scene from inside Hagia Sophia

View of the east wall of the south gallery

Image of the Madonna and Child in the Apse of Hagia Sophia.

narthex is an image of the Virgin Mary sitting in a throne with the child Jesus sitting in her lap. Emperor Constantine I (324-337), with a model of the city in his hand is on the left with the motto, "Great Emperor Constantine among the Saints", while on the right is an image of Justinian, holding a model of Hagia Sophia with the motto, "Emperor Justinian whose memory is famous". The bronze door ornamented with relief motifs under this mosaic originally belonged to a pagan temple in Tarsus, dating back to the 2nd century BC, and was brought and placed here by Emperor Theophilus (829-842) in the year 838. On the apse of the church there is a mosaic of the Madonna and Child accompanied by the Archangel Gabriel, along with images of Saints John Chrysostom, Ignatius the Younger and Ignatius Theophorus, all identified by name. There is also an image

Detail from the vestibule door

of the Emperor Alexandrus (912-913) in the northern gallery. In the southern gallery there is a Deesis mosaic of Jesus, flanked by the Virgin Mary on the left and by John the Baptist on the right. In front of the wall right opposite this mosaic there is an epigraph indicating the tomb of the Venetian Doge Henricus Dandolo, who played a role in the taking of Constantinople from the Byzantine Empire,

View of the ceiling of Hagia Sophia

and who died here. Also in this gallery, a series of Viking inscriptions can be seen on the marble balustrade. On the left hand side of the southern gallery's eastern wall there is a triptych mosaic, consisting of Jesus in the middle, Emperor Constantine Monomachus (1042-1055) on the left with the inscription, "Constantine Monochamus, by the Divine Christ, Faithful King of the Romans", and Em-

press Zoe on the right with the inscription, "The Very Religious Augusta Zoe". On the right hand side of this same wall is another mosaic of the Madonna and Child, to the left of whom is Emperor John II Comnenus (1118-1143) with the inscription, "Porphyrogenitus John Comnenus, Emperor of the Romans", while on the right is Empress Eirene with their son Alexius, inscribed, "The Religious Augusta Eirene".

The mosaics of Hagia Sophia, which was converted to a mosque with the conquest of Istanbul, were plastered over in the 16th Century. The mosaics were revealed upon removal of the plaster during extensive restoration work by the Swiss Fossatti brothers in the reign of Sultan Abdülmecit (1839-1861), carried out between 1847 and 1849. Although Sultan Abdülmecit wanted the mosaics to remain in the open, he had to have them plastered over again because of the reactions of religious fanatics. American Thomas Wittermore again uncovered the mosaics as a result of works carried out in 1932. Additions were made during the Ottoman era; such as a niche, pulpit and muezzin's lodge during the reign of Sultan Murat III (1574-1595), a library during Mahmut I's (1730-1754) reign, a Sultan's Lodge and Sultan's

View of the Deisis mosaic in the South Gallery

Pavilion during that of Abdülmecit. Circular panels with the names, written in Arabic, of God, Mohammed, the four Caliphs along with Hassan and Hussein were hung up in the building, and a verse of the Koran, taken from sura of Nur (Heavenly Light) was inscribed on the main dome by the calligrapher Kazasker (a military judge) Mustafa İzzet Effendi. On the main floor are two marble urns of the Hellenistic period which were brought from Pergamum. On the buildings exterior a brick minaret was added during the reign of Fatih, another one during that of Beyazit II, and the two western minarets are the work of the architect Mimar Sinan. In the garden of Hagia Sophia can be found; the fountain and Boys' School constructed in 1740 by Sultan Mahmut I, the Muvakkithane (rooms of the Timekeeper, who

determined the times of prayer, etc.), constructed by Abdülmecit in 1853, and ruins of madrasah from the reign of Fatih.

The mausoleum of Selim II, one of the ottoman sultans, built by Mimar Sinan, as well as the Mausoleum of Princes; the mausoleum of Murat III built by the architect Davut Agha; and the mausoleum of Mehmet III, built by Dalgıç (Diver) Mehmet Agha, can all be found in the southern court of Hagia Sophia. Besides these, the mausoleums of Sultan Mustafa I and Sultan Ibrahim are in the Baptistery.

Hagia Sophia was converted to a museum by order of President Mustafa Kemal Atatürk and decree number 2/1589 of the Council of Ministers under the chairmanship of Prime Minister İsmet İnönu on November 24th, 1934, and was opened to the public on February 1st, 1935 under the name of "Museum of Hagia Sophia".

Image of Jesus and John Prodromos (Baptist Yahya) on the panel of the Deisis mosaic

02 AYA IRINI

Exterior view of Aya Irini

The church of Aya Irini in the external court of Topkapı Palace and inside Sur-u Sultan-i was constructed during the reign of Constantine I (306-337). Aya Irini means "Sacred Peace". It is one of the oldest churches from the Byzantine era in Istanbul. The second Ecumenical Council Meeting, held in 381 in Istanbul, was convened in the church of Aya Irini. The church was largely burnt and collapsed during the Nika rebellion in 532. Emperor Justinian I (527-565) had the church rebuilt in a short time and it was opened for worship, possibly in the year 548. The church was extensively damaged by the earthquakes that happened in the 9th century.

Aya Irini is the biggest church in Istanbul after Hagia Sophia. The church has the appearance of basilical structure, consisting of atrium, narthex and main floor with three naves, apse and galleries. Once ascends bilateral wooden stairs from the main floor to the galleries. Including the atrium the church measures 100x32 meters. The main floor of the church alone measures 43x57 meters. The main floor is

General view of Aya Irini

General Scene from inside Aya Irini

Photo by Tahsin Aydoğmuş

General view of the south façade of Aya Irini

separated into three naves by columns and ranks and is covered by domes and vaults. The main dome is 15 meters in diameter and its elevation from the floor is 35 meters. An emblem containing weapons was inscribed in the middle of the dome during the ottoman era. The three-windowed apse is covered by a semi-dome, on which is a cross with three large arms on a gilded background. On the arc of the apse a piece, consisting of two lines taken from the Torah, is written in letters set in mosaic. One passes from the narthex to the atrium of the church through five doors. The atrium is surrounded by porticos with vaulted arches, and was narrowed by the addition of a series of porticos in the ottoman era. Aya Irini is the only remaining church from the Byzantine period to have an atrium. It is believed that the interior of the church was richly decorated, however earthquakes, destruction by the hand of man, and other natural disasters caused marble coatings and mosaic deco-

rations to vanish.

After the conquest of Istanbul the church was not converted to a mosque, but was used as a weapons cache or "arsenal" (cebehane) and for appropriated goods, subsequently becoming a place for the exhibition of various weapons during the reign of Sultan Ahmet III (1703-1730). Ahmet Fethi Pasha, Marshall of Tophane, formed the core of the first Turkish Museum in Aya Irini in 1846. Archaeological and ethnographical creations were also

A moment from a concert at Aya Irini

Photo by Tahsin Aydoğmuş

View of the entrance dome

exhibited in the museum. When the Museum of Aya Irini was nominated the Imperial Museum (Muze-I Hümayun) in 1869, it couldn't meet its requirements, so the pieces were moved to Çinili Köşk (Ceramics Villa) in 1875. Aya Irini, which served as a Military Museum from 1908, was emptied and handed over to the Ministry of Arts and Culture following the removal of the Military Museum to Harbiye in 1978. Today, it is open to visitors as a memorial museum and hosts different cultural and social activities.

View of Aya Irini's apse and main dome

Main entrance door of Aya Irini

03 SMALL HAGIA SOPHIA MOSQUE

Church of Saint Sergios and Bakhos

This church is situated between the Cankurtaran and Kadırga districts in Eminönü. According to rumour, when Justinian I (512-527) was facing punishment for his participation in a rebellion against his uncle, Emperor Justin I (527-565), Saint Sergios and Bakhos appeared to the latter in a dream to give evidence on behalf of the former and thus he was spared. When Justinian became Emperor and ascended to the throne, he had Small Hagia Sophia Church constructed on behalf of these saints in order to pay his debt of gratitude.

The church was constructed by Emperor Justinian I and Empress Theodora in the years 527-536 on behalf of Saint Sergios and Bakhos. It is a small version of

the great Hagia Sophia church in Istanbul. The main floor of the church is on a square plan and covered by a main dome with eight angles sitting on eight pillars. Its apse protrudes externally and is covered by a semi-dome. The church consists of the main floor, the narthex, and the galleries. One ascends from the narthex to the galleries, which surround the interior on three sides. The southern gallery was kept larger than the northern one. All the way around the building's interior, on the architraves surmounting the pillars on the ground floor is an epitaph indicating that the church was dedicated to Saint Sergios and Bakhos by Emperor Justinian and Empress Theodora. Sixteen red and green porphyry columns were used on the ground floor and eighteen in the galleries. The monograms of Emperor Justinian were engraved on the capitals of the basket-shaped columns in the lower floor.

There was originally an atrium (court) in front of the church. According to the epigraph mounted on its door in the ottoman era, the church was converted to a mosque and small dervish lodge between the years 1500 and 1505 by Hussein Agha, the Agha of Darüssaade (Chief Eunuch at the Palace), during the reign of Sultan Beyazit II (1481-1512). The marble niche and pulpit inside the mosque date from the early 16th century. After its conversion to mosque, a final congregation area, with six columns and five domes with arcade, was appended to the western side of the structure. In place of the atrium (court) a small dervish lodge was also constructed. At the south western

corner of the mosque, the minaret standing apart from the main building was constructed by Grand Vizier Ahmet Pasha after 1750, having built the fountain and school in 1740. In 1936, for reasons unknown, the minaret was demolished from the rostrum upwards and was reconstructed from hewed stone. Finally, the tomb of Hussein Agha can be found at the northern side of the mosque.

04 HARUTIUM (SURP) CHURCH

This church is in Çakmaktaş Street, Şehsuvarbey quarter, Kumkapı, in Eminönü district. Some of the Armenians brought to Istanbul during the reign of Fatih Sultan Mehmet were placed in the Kumkapi quarter. In order to meet the need for worship of the people of this district, in the course of time a chapel was constructed here named "Camp of Clerygmen Baptism Room" by the firman of sultan, dated 1832. Later on, Kazaz Artin (Harutyum Amira Bezciyan) enlarged and converted the chapel into a church by a second firman that he got from the Palace, and he had a school constructed for poor children beside it. The current church was constructed in 1855. The belfry of the church was restored in 1907.

The church, built to a rectangular plan in the court was constructed in an east-west orientation. One enters from the main door to the narthex. The lateral parts of the narthex, built to a rectangular plan in a north-south orientation, are a step higher than the middle part. There is a gallery, in which the church organ can be found, over the narthex whose ceiling is flat. It is separated from the main floor by iron cages. One passes through the arched and iron fenced door to the main floor. The ceiling covering of the church is barrel vaulted. The apse extends externally and is covered by a semi-dome. The section allocated to the

choir and the spirituals, which is separated from the main floor by wooden fences, is a step higher than the main floor. There is a small room along each side of this section. The northern room is used as a baptistery and the southern room is used as a dressing room of the spirituals.

The apse is three steps higher than the dais section, and one ascends to the apse by stairs on either side. The altar is in the middle of the apse.

05 PANAYIA ELPIDA CHURCH

This church is in a court surrounded by high walls between Müsteşar, Gerdanlık, and Samsa Streets in Kumkapi, in Eminönü district. There is a holy spring of the orthodox Greeks to which one descends by a set of stairs in the basement at the south–eastern end of the building.

It is understood from several ruins existing here that there was an old building there in the 15th century. S. Gerlach attended a ceremony conducted by the Patriarch in the church in 1576 and talked about the icons in this church. The church takes its place in the lists of Tryphon in 1583 and Paterakis in 1604. The church, largely damaged in the fire of 1660, was reconstructed in 1680. It appears in the map of Fr. Kauffer, dated 1776, by the name of "Panaia tis Elpidos". Furthermore, it was denoted as "Greek Church" on the croquis dated 1875, of the Municipality.

The church was constructed in an east-west orientation with a rectangular plan. Three apses extend eastwards.

The apse in the middle axis is big; the ones on the other sides are small. Westwards, on the northern and southern corners, there are two belfries of the baldachin type. The dome above the central floor sits upon a tambour frame fixed on four columns. Vertical cross arms in four directions at this place are covered with cross vaults. The building was constructed with smooth hewn stone. The exterior sides show similarities to one another.

The church is of closed Greek cross plan. The main floor is bounded by three round apses of which the one in the eastern axis is deeper, and with a rectangular narthex in a north-south orientation. The dais is three steps higher than the ground. The gallery on the narthex reaches to the line of western columns. One ascends to the gallery through stone stairs in the southern corner of the narthex. Four columns in the main floor and two columns in the west are connected to each other by round arches. There are also three niches in each of, the middle and northern apses at the east end of the main floor,

two small niches in the southern apse, and also two small niches to the south of the dais. The main altar is in the middle of the apse on the middle axis. Marble iconostasis can be seen in line with square sectioned columns in the east of the main floor.

At the north end of the main floor both, the marble ambon sitting on the second column supporting the dome, and the despot throne in front of the column opposite, are decorated, in sculpture and relief, with herbal motifs.

06 KIRYAKI (AYIA) CHURCH

The church situated between Gedik Pasha Stret, Çadırcı Mosque Street, and Kadirga Harbour Street in the district of Kumkapi is surrounded by high walls and stands in a court to which one ascends by stair. One descends to a holy spring of the Greek orthodox of Ayios Vasiliyos (Saint Basil), situated in the basement, through the stairs in the south western corner of the church. Although the exact construction date of the church is not known, the name of the church is in the lists prepared by Tryphon in 1583 and Paterakis in 1604. The church was restored in 1730. It appeared also by the name of "Aia Kirlaki" in the Kauffer map, dated 1776. The current church was constructed by the Karaman community between the years 1895-1901, in place of a collapsed church. The architect of the church is Periklifo Tiadis.

It is a structure of a rectangular central planned type, whose main floor is covered by a dome with high tambour frame, including windows, which sits on eight columns. Three semi-

ΕΙΣΕΛΕΥΣΟΜΑΙ ΕΙΣ ΤΟΝ ΟΙΚ
ΣΟΥ ΠΡΟΣΚΥΝΗΣΩ ΠΡΟΣ ΝΑΟΝ ΑΓΙΟΝ ΣΟΥ ΚΥΡΙΕ

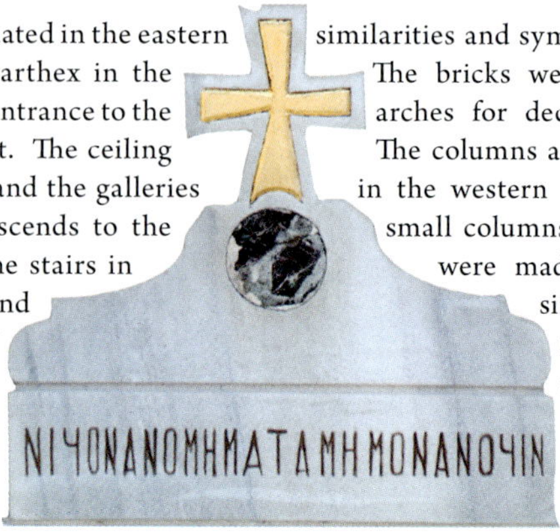

rounded apses are situated in the eastern axis; a rectangular narthex in the west. There is a triad entrance to the narthex from the west. The ceiling of the narthex is flat and the galleries are above it. One ascends to the galleries by way of the stairs in the south western and north western ends of the main floor. One climbs three steps to the apse section. The apses are covered with a semi-dome. Reciprocal entrances appear at each of the northern and southern ends of the dais. There is a single entrance from the narthex to the main floor. At the western end of the structure, belfries of the baldachin shape extend from the northern and southern facades.

Hewn stone was used as the construction material. The sides of the church show similarities and symmetry dominates. The bricks were placed on the arches for decorative purposes. The columns and arches situated in the western entrance, and the small columns on the windows, were made of marble. A single line of tooth motif in brick surrounds the whole structure on the underside of the stoa. The paving of the main floor is marble.

The wooden ambon in the church is of baldachin type. The despot throne is made of wood. A marble iconostasis appears between the naves and the apse. There is an image of "Jesus the Pantocrator" on the medallion in the middle of the main dome, an image of "The Virgin Mary of Blachernae" on the dome of the

apse, scenes taken from the Bible on the southern and northern walls of the main floor, and depictions that include subjects taken from the Torah on the narthex.

07 ASDVADZADZIN (SURP) CHURCH

The church situated at Şarapnel Street in Kumkapi is known as the Church or Cathedral of the Patriarch. It is one of a number of Byzantine churches that were given to the Armenian community after the conquest of Istanbul. Although its first construction date is not known, Simon the Pole mentions it in his travel book in 1608. In 1641 the Chair of the Armenian Patriarch and the Patriarchate were moved from Samatya to Kumkapi.

The Patriarchate and the Church underwent regular restorations in 1819 because of the fires it experienced in the years 1718 and 1762. The Patriarchate was completely burnt in the fire of 1826. Construction work was commenced by the firman of Sultan, obtained in the same year. Krikor Amira Balyan and Dövletyan Garabed drew the plans for the church complex. A classroom for poor children and two classrooms for theology education were constructed, as well as three big and three small churches and chapels. A clock tower was constructed at the main entrance of the Cathedral in 1870.

Asdvadzadzin church, situated in a court surrounded by high walls, is a typical basilical structure in an east-west orientation. One enters the church underneath the western belfry. The narthex section is divided into three naves by three columns adjacent to the wall. The lateral naves of the narthex are two steps higher than the middle nave. The ceiling in the middle nave is barrel-vaulted; the ceilings of the lateral naves are planar. The tomb of Patriarch Nerses II Varjabedyan is in the south western corner of the narthex. One passes to the main church, onto the main floor through the grilled door at the end of the narthex. The main floor is divided into three naves by a series of six columns bound to each other by arches.

The section starting from the line of the last columns in the middle nave and ending by the apse is allocated to the choir and the spirituals. The Patriarch's and Bishop's thrones are in this section, separated by high barriers. One climbs five steps to the apse. There are small altars next to the main altar, which is situated in the middle of the apse. The ambon is on the wall of the northern nave; again there are thrones of the Patriarchate and the Bishop in the area allocated to the spirituals, in front of the line of northward columns. The middle nave of the main floor is barrel-vaulted and the lateral naves are covered by planar ceilings.

One passes from the northern nave to Surp Harutyun Church and Surp Khaç Church, and from the southern nave to the Baptistery Church of Surp Dzınunt. Surp Haturyan Church is of the basilical plan and is covered by a vault. The bust and tomb of Harutyun Amira Bezciyan are in the north western corner of this church. One descends to the holy spring of Surp Theodoros through stairs by the tomb. The churches of Surp Khaç and Vortvos Vorodman are two symmetrical structures. The main entrance door of the Church of Surp Khaç is westwards. Columns adjacent to both walls are lined up after the entrance. As opposed to the cathedral it has a "U" shaped gallery, generally allocated to the choir, which sits on the first ten columns. A door opens to the corridor at the south eastern end of the Church of Vortvos Vorodman. Another door opens to the garden in the south eastern corner. There are also two more altars at both sides of the main altar in the apse.

The Armenian Patriarchate is at the west of the church and the Armenian School is to the north.

MERYEM ANA
ERMENİ KİLİSESİ
Ս.ԱՍՏՈՒԱԾԱԾԻՆ
ՄԱՅՐ ԵԿԵՂԵՑԻ

08 HOVHANNES AVEDARANİÇ (SURP) CHURCH

Originally built of wood on the same site in 1827, this church is located on Sarayiçi Street, in the Şehsuvar quarter of Gedikpaşa district. It is a Gregorian Armenian church. In 1849, 22 years after it was opened for worship, the church was burnt down. Rebuilt according to the firman in 1871 of Sultan Abdülaziz (1861-1876), it was reopened for worship in 1876.

It was extensively restored in 1895, during the reign of Patriarch Mattheus of Izmir. For many years after this date the church was neglected until it was

restored in 1950-1951, suffered great damage in a fire in 1972, and was restored anew in 1975. The fully restored church was reopened to prayer with a ceremony in 1986.

Surrounded by walls and houses, the church is built on an east-west orientation. The narthex entrance is directly after the small windbreaker at the western end. Built to a north-south rectangular plan and in three sections, the lateral sections of the narthex are two steps higher than the central section. There is a gallery above the flat-ceilinged narthex. The narthex leads to the main floor (nave). The main floor and the gallery are cradle-vaulted.

The north and south walls are brightened by three opposing windows on

each. At the front of the main floor is the area belonging to the choir and the spirituals. The door opening to the north from this area leads to the baptistery and the treasury room, while the southward door leads to the priests' and cantors' changing rooms. The semi-circular apse is covered by a semi-dome and is accessed by three steps on either side. There is a magnificent altar in the centre of the apse. There is a belfry tower on the roof directly above the church building's western entrance. In the church courtyard can be found administration buildings belonging to the church management.

09 MOSQUE OF BODRUM

Mirelaion Monastery Church

The Mosque of Bodrum, situated at the south end of Ordu Street in Laleli is an old Byzantine church, and is known as Mosque of Mesih Pasha because of the name of its founder. The church was constructed by Romanus Lecapenus I (920-944), as the Monastery Church of Mirelaion. The Monastery of Mirelaion was a monastery for women. The monastery had experienced a fire during Latin occupation (1204-1261).

The church stood empty for some time after the conquest of Istanbul, and was converted to a mosque by Grand Vizier Mesih Ali Pahsa in 1501. It was called Mosque of Bodrum (Basement) because of the existence of a large water cistern beneath the structure. The building was

largely damaged by fire in 1782 and 1911 and stayed like that for years. The historic building was rescued from this condition by restoration in 1986.

The church, constructed over a cellar was made of brick. The church was constructed to a plan of closed cross shape with four supports. One passes a three sectioned narthex at the entrance, into the main floor. The main floor is covered by a tambour framed dome that includes high windows. Four ranks, on which the pendentives that provide the entrance are located, are crude supports made of stone. There were columns in place of these supports in the original structure. The apse, which is semi rounded on the inside, and three sided on the outside, is on the western side of the structure. There are cells at both sides of the structure. The walls of the structure were supported by semi rounded supports on the exterior facades. The minaret in the corner to the right hand side of the entrance is completely made of stone.

10 THE MOSQUE OF KALENDERHANE

This church, situated where the Street of Bozdoğan and the Street of March 16th Martyrs intersect in Vezneciler quarter in Eminönü district, was converted to a mosque. The exact construction date of the church is not known. It was suggested that it was previously the church of Diakonissa and latterly the Monastery Church of Akataleotos. After the conquest of Istanbul the church, initially allocated to the Kalenderi cult as a small dervish lodge, was later converted to a mosque. It is the most important example of the cross shape within a square plan amongst Byzantine architectural structures.

After excavations, the construction of a central-planned new church was started, possibly in the 8th century, on the ruins of an old church. The church of the most recent period was exactly like a classical period Byzantine church with its cross-shaped main floor, lateral naves, narthex, and the gallery above it. It had an iconostasis separating the dais from the main floor rising to the gallery floor.

It was allocated to catholic Italians during the Latin invasion (1204-1261). Frescoes from the life of Saint Francesco were found in the church. The structure had experienced various changes during the Byzantine period.

Because of that, the church has a very complex plan.

The church was previously used as a small dervish lodge during the ottoman era. The apse section of the structure collapsed when it was converted to a mosque by Maktul Beşir Agha, the Agha of Darüssaade, in the first half of the 18th century, and the structure was largely damaged after the earthquake of 1720, and the fires of 1718 and 1727. The semi-rounded part of the apse was closed with a planar wall. The current niche was constructed on this wall. The room in the south western corner of the main floor was filled in and the minaret was constructed on it. The restorations that were made during the ottoman era destroyed several architectural characteristics of the structure. The mosque which was

used until the 1930's was deserted after this date. Detailed archeological studies were carried out in Kalenderhane between the years of 1966-1975. The structure, which had lost its originality due to interferences performed in the past, has been successfully restored by adhering to the original during the latest restoration works.

11

CHURCH MOSQUE OF VEFA
The Church of Thedoros (Ayios)

The church situated in the street of Molla Şemseddin Mosque in Vefa district is accepted as most probably being the Church of Saint Theodoros. It is also known as Church Mosque of Vefa in order to distinguish it from the Mosque of Molla Gürani, the Mosque of Molla Şemseddin and other neighbouring mosques.

Theodoros was a soldier commissioned by the Roman Army who was killed because he accepted Christianity. He was ordained a saint later on. It is thought that the church was constructed in the 10th or 11th centuries. The structure was modelled as a four columned closed Greek cross. Its main floor is covered by a windowed high dome with tambour frame. When the previous four columns in the

main floor were damaged by fire, unfeatured supports were put in their place during the restoration. At the eastern end of the church an apse protrudes externally with vaulted cells at the sides of this apse. There is a three-sectioned narthex at the western side of the main floor.

After the rescue of the city from Latin invasion in 1261, the church underwent a great restoration and the exterior narthex

forming the current entrance was added to the structure. Mosaic pictures found on the domes of the exterior narthex during the investigations made here in 1937 were demolished in recent years.

The apse wall of the church that was converted to a mosque by Molla Gürani was engraved and made into a niche.

Furthermore, the minaret was constructed on the thick wall on the right hand side.

12 MOSQUE OF FENARI ISA
Monastry Church of Konstantinos Lips

The mosque of Fenari Isa situated on the coast of Vatan Street in Fatih quarter is a Byzantine structure which was converted from a church. The structure consists of two adjacent churches constructed in two different periods and the parecclesion, which was added later on. The church at the northern end was constructed in 907 as a monastery church by Constantine Lips, the fleet admiral, during the reign of Emperor Leo VI (886-912).

A second church was constructed on

behalf of John Prodromos by Theodora, the wife of Emperor Michael VIII (1261-1282), adjacent to the southern side of the church. Because the church was designed for the tombs of the dynastic family, several personages belonging to the dynasty were buried here. There are tombs under both buildings and the pavements of the parecclesion.

The church was converted to a mosque at the end of the 15th century by Alaeddin Ali Efendi of the Fenarizades, one of the famous ulema families. A brick minaret was also added to the south western corner of the structure. The mosque was later named Mosque of Fenari Isa because of the title of the ulema's family.

The north church was planned in the shape of a four columned Greek cross that follows the narthex. There is a Greek epigraph showing that the church is dedicated to the Virgin Mary on the marble arch that rounds on the bulges of the apse. The northern wall of the structure was completely reconstructed. The windows and tambour-framed domes of both churches underwent restoration.The columns were removed and big arches were constructed in their place in order to make the main

floor more usable. This section underwent two big fires in 1633 and 1918.
In the south church, the main floor following the narthex was constructed according to a system known as gallery-type.

A tambour-framed dome covers the top of the central area which rises as a square mass. An additional building (pareccleσion) surrounding both churches from the south eastern direction was constructed in the 14th century.

13 MONASTERY OF STUDIUS
Church Of John (Ayıos) Prodromos
(Mosque of Imrahor İlyas Bey)

The Church of John the Baptist (Baptizer Yahya), situated in Imrahor Street in Yedikule forms a part of the Monastery of Studius. The church, which is in a very ruined condition, is one of the oldest buildings in Istanbul. The church

of John Prodromos was constructed between the years 454 and 463 as a big monastery on land belonging to the Eastern Consul, Studius himself, who bore the title of patrician during the reign of Emperor Leo I (457-474). The monastery maintained its importance as a prominent religious centre in the Byzantine era. Famous patriarchs were educated here. It became a tradition for the emperors to pray here when entering the city by the Golden Gate.

The Monastery and the Church were plundered and largely damaged during the Latin invasion (1204-1261) at the time of the Fourth Crusade. The church was largely restored in 1293 by Constantine Palaeologus, the brother of Emperor Andronicus II (1282-1328), and it was encompassed by thick walls. Excursionists who came to Istanbul in the 13th and 15th centuries talk about the decoration and the grandiose appearance of the church.

The church is a successful example of Hellenistic type basilicas in terms of plan. One passes from the atrium to the three-sectioned narthex after the colonnade with four marble columns. At the right hand side of the narthex, there is a brick minaret, which is ruined from the minaret balcony up. Five doors lead from

the narthex to the main floor. The main floor was divided longitudinally into three naves by lines of columns, seven on each side. The whole column-series on the right hand side was destroyed by fires and earthquakes. Six columns remain standing from the column-series on the left hand side. It is understood that there were galleries above the lateral naves to which one ascends from the narthex. One can see interconnected rich marble flooring decorations on the floor of the middle nave, which were possibly made in the 13th century.

The church was converted to a mosque by Imrahor Ilyas Bey and named the Mosque of Imrahor Ilyas Bey during the reign of Sultan Bayezit II (1481-1512) after the conquest of Istanbul. The mosque, which experienced a fire in 1782, was largely damaged in 1894 due to an earthquake. The roof of the mosque, unable to bear the weight of snow collapsed, and

the structure, which couldn't be restored again, became ruined and reached its current state. Today, it serves as a memorial museum bound to the Directorship of the Hagia Sophia Museum of Istanbul.

There is a reservoir that belongs to this monastery some distance from the Monastery of Studius. There is a holy spring with an apse and two columns that was constructed adjacent to this reservoir, and is partly ruined. This holy spring is one of the oldest holy springs of the Byzantine period.

14 MOSQUE OF GREAT MUSTAPHA PASHA
Andreas (Ayios) Monastery Church

The church, situated in Kocamustafapaşa quarter, was converted to a church from Ayios Andreas (Saint Andrew) Monastery dating from the 6th and 7th centuries. The church, restored by Emperor Basil I (867-886), was largely ruined during the Latin invasion of 1204-1261. Ayios Andreas Monastery Church, of gallery type and renewed in about 1284 by Protovestiarissa Theodora Raouleina, the nephew of Byzantine Emperor Michael Palaeologus VIII (1259-1282), using old materials, was converted to a mosque by Grand Vizier Great Mustapha Pasha in 1489-91. It is also known as Sümbül Effendi Mosque.

There also is, within the complex of buildings adjacent to the mosque (Külliye),

structures such as madrasah, Turkish bath, muvakkithane (rooms of the Timekeeper), the tomb of Sümbül Effendi, the tomb of commander-in-chief Rıza Pasha, the tomb of Safiye Hanim, double tomb of Sultans, chamber of the tomb caretaker (türbedar), the fountain of Hadji Başir Agha, and the public fountain of Emine Hanim.

Ayios Andreas Church is a cross-planned church. Its dome sits on four columns. Its column capitals are monogrammed.

It has three apses and two narthexes.

Today, the only remains from the monastery complex are the monastery of the church that was converted to mosque. When the church, constructed to an east-west orientation, was converted to a mosque, a new axis in a north-south orientation was given to the building for the purpose of worship. The western entrance was closed for this purpose.

A niche was constructed on the southern wall of the main floor. A window was opened from the middle of the apse in an eastern direction. The minaret of the mosque was constructed in front of the western wall. Profound architectural changes have been made inside and outside of the building. A final congregation area with five domes was added to the

north end of the structure and entrance to the mosque was from this direction. There is a marble epigraph, on which there are two sultan's signatures belonging to Sultan Mahmut II (1808-1839), in the central part of the niche situated in the final congregation area.

Indeed, the Byzantine structure was predisposed to Turkish architecture. The unique characteristic showing that the structure is a Byzantine church is the element that exceeds the level of the lead-coated roof at the eastern end, and that covers the cradle vault of the semi dome of the main apse.

15 KEVORK (SURP) CHURCH

The church situated in Marmara Street in Kocamustafapaşa is referred to by the names of; "Teotokos", "Perivleptos", "Ayia Panayia", "Panayia Perivleptos" during the Byzantine era; "Aqueous Monastery" during the ottoman period; and is referred to by Armenians by the names of "Surp Asdvadzadzin" and "Surp Kevork".

The first church was constructed in the year 1031 by order of the Emperor Romanus III (1028-1034). The church was pillaged by Venetians during the Latin invasion of 1204. It was restored and opened for worship during the reign of Emperor Michael Palaeologus VIII (1261-1282) after the invasion. The church was allocated to the Armenians by or-

der of Fatih in 1461 after the conquest of Istanbul. It was nicknamed "Bloody Church" because it caused bloody events between Armenians and Greek Turks who didn't accept it.
The church became "Surp Asdvadzadzin" after being given to the Armenians. The appearance of a reservoir next to the holy spring, a Greek Church tradition, caused Turks to name it the "Aqueous Monastery".

The church was largely damaged in by fire in 1660 and was reconstructed in 1722. At this time, a chapel named Surp Yerrortutyun was added. It was constructed again in 1804 by Hagop Amira Güllapyan and Minas Kalfa. It experienced another fire in 1782. The church, having undergone restoration in 1831 and 1843, was ruined extensively in the fire of 1866. The church was reconstructed under the direction of Architect Bedros Nemtze between the years 1885 and 1843 and was opened for worship. The church, restored after the earthquake of 1894, was restored again because of the fire in 1895. Later, having been used for military purposes during the First World War (1914-1918), the church was again opened for worship after the Armistice of Mondros. The church was damaged during the events of 6-7 September 1955.

It experienced a fire in 1960 and was restored in 1963. The latest restoration was made to the church in 1993.

Although the church has a basilical plan, it became a Greek cross with the chapels that were constructed northwards and southwards. One enters the narthex from the main gate to the west. The lateral sections of the narthex are three steps higher than the middle section. There is an altar adjacent to the wall in the southern section that was dedicated to Saint Kevork. One enters the main floor from the narthex by passing through an iron-grilled door. There is a large gallery with three steps allocated to the choir above the narthex. The main floor is covered with barrel vault. The area elevated by one step at the east of the main floor is allocated to the choir and the spirituals.

There is a throne allocated to the Patriarch. This section is separated from the area where worship is performed by wooden barriers. One passes to the chapels by doors in the north and south of this section. The apse is elevated by four steps above this section. The main altar, made of wood and of high artistic value, is in the centre of the apse covered by a semi dome. There is a small altar in each of the niches to both sides. The two chapels, of basilical type, are covered with cross like vaults. The chapel in the north is used as a baptistery.

The belfry appears above the main entrance gate of the church. The main two-doored entrance gate of the church is made of iron and is extremely ornamented. Scenes relating to the life of Saint Kevork, after whom the church is named, appear on the gate. The holy spring and Armenian School are located at the west of the church.

16 CONSTANTINE (AYIOS) Eleni (AYIA) Church

It is situated in the middle of a large court, surrounded by Imrahor Ilyas Bey Street, Feridun Kılıç Street, and Church Street, between Samatya and Yedikule. There is a belfry of baldachin type at the north of the court and social facilities and administration buildings appear at its southern end. It is believed that the relic of the emperor's arm and hand is hidden in the church, which is sanctified on behalf of Constantine I (324-337) and his mother Helena during the Byzantine period.

This church is known as the church of Karamanians because of the fact that Greek Turks from Karaman, who settled here during the migrations following the conquest of Istanbul, constructed it on old ruins by permission of Fatih Sultan Mehmet (1451-1481). The name of the church is mentioned in literature of the 15th and 17th centuries. The church experienced a fire in 1689 and was restored again. The church,

rebuilt and opened to visitors in 1805, underwent a restoration under the direction of the architect Constantine in 1833. The church was renewed in 1963.

The church was built to a rectangular plan and was constructed in an east-west orientation. The apse in the eastern axis is protrudes outside and has nine sides. There is an additional area in a rectangular plan adjacent to the church's southern end. The main floor of the church, of basilical plan type, has three naves. There is a narthex with rectangular plan at the entrance and a semi-rounded apse at the east of the middle nave. There are six lines of columns between the naves. The lateral naves are one step higher than the middle nave. The dais aligned with the first columns at the east of the main floor is one step higher than the lateral naves and two steps higher than the middle

nave. There is a rectangular planned gallery above the western narthex. The covering system of the church is concrete, the ceiling of the middle nave is low vault, and the lateral naves and narthex are flat-ceilinged.
Furthermore, the ceiling of the narthex was divided into five parts. The inner cover of the apse is a semi-dome.
There are two entrances to the narthex, from the north and the west. However, there are three entrances from the narthex to the main floor. There is a small entrance at each of the south and the north ends of the dais. The wooden iconostasis including three naves at the east of the main floor, the wooden ambon which sits on the third column from the east of the northern carrier line, and opposite it the despot throne at the southern side are ornamented with herbal motifs of sculpture and relief technique.

17 PANAYIA BELGRADU CHURCH

It is situated in a court surrounded by high walls in Hadji Hamza Street in Belgradkapi in Fatih district. There is a holy spring of the same name at the south of the court. The church is located in the quarter in which the Christians brought from Belgrade were placed after the annexation of Belgrade to ottoman territories in 1521, and referred to as "Belgradkapı" today, and was constructed in 1523.

Again, the church was dedicated to Ayia Praskevi because of the relic and icons of Saint Paraskevi that these immigrants brought with them during the years of the church's construction. After the removal of the relics that were in the church to Pammakaristos Monastery in 1539, the church was dedicated to the Virgin Mary.

The church was constructed in an east-west orientation and is built to a rectangular plan. The main floor of the church is of basilical plan type and has three naves. The apse in line with the middle nave is deep and round.

However, the narthex is built to a rectangular plan in a north-south orientation. There are four lines of columns between each of the naves. The platform in front of the main floor is one step higher than the lateral naves and two steps higher than the middle nave. The gallery is above the narthex. One ascends to the gallery by stairs situated in the southern part

of the narthex. The cover system of the church is barrel vault on the naves and flat ceiling on the narthex. The church is covered by double-faced ribbed roof on the outside and the roof of the apse is semi conical. The interior cover of the protruding part of the apse is a semi-dome. Three doors open to the main floor from the narthex in line with the naves.

The apse has three niches. There are also two small niches at each of the right and the left of the apse. The altar appears in the middle of the apse. The iconostasis comprises of three naves at the east of the main floor. The wooden ambon that sits on the second column from the front of the northern column line, and the despot throne opposite it are ornamented with herbal motifs of sculpture and relief technique.

18 NIGOĞAYOS (SURP) CHURCH

It is situated in the corner where Sulukule Street and Karatay Street intersect in Topkapi in Fatih district. It is known that a wooden church was constructed between the years 1626 and 1630. This church was restored, by Vartan Kalfa, in the years 1813 and 1823 by a firman dated 1811. The church was pulled down by the firman dated 1831 of Mahmut II (1808-1839), reconstructed by Vartan Kalfa Tıngıryan and opened for worship in 1832. The church was damaged by the earthquake of 1894, was restored, and opened for worship in the same year. The church was largely damaged while being used for military purposes during the First World War. Extensively restored during the reign of the Turkish Republic, the church was opened again to visitors in 1927. The church was finally restored in 1983.

The narthex situated at the west of the church is built to a rectangular plan in a north-south orientation, and opens eastwards to the nave. The narthex, above which there is a gallery, has a flat wooden roof. The apse at the east of the nave is semi rounded inside and protrudes. One ascends to the apse from both sides via three steps each. The main altar is in the middle of the apse and on each side there is one small altar. The door which opens to the north from the area belonging to the choir and the spirituals goes to the baptistery room, and the door which opens to the south goes to the dressing room of the chorists. The belfry appears at the southwest of the church. The church has a barrel vault shaped wooden roof inside. It is covered by double-faced joint roof on the outside.

19 ZOODOHOS PIYI CHURCH

Panagia Pege "Paella" Church

It is situated next to the Greek orthodox cemetery in Kazlıçeşme in Zeytinburnu district. The church appears in the middle of a court surrounded by high walls. The holy spring bearing the same name as the church is adjacent to its north western corner. Deceased orthodox patriarchs and some major religious personages are buried in the west of the court. The sources that give information about the history of the church compose myths related to the belief that it was established on "life-giving source", which is also the meaning of its name, and the miracles of this source. The history of the church dates back to the 5th and 6th centuries. The church, constructed by the emperor Leo I (457-474), was enlarged during the reign of Emperor Justinian I (527-565).

The church was damaged as a result of earthquakes which happened in Istanbul, and was restored in 790 by Eirene and in 870 by the emperor Basil I. Again, the church was restored by Romanus Lecapenus I (920-944), because of the fire the church had experienced. The church went though the Latin invasion (1204-1261), along with the city in 1204. The church was largely damaged while Ottoman Sultan Murat I (1421-1451) used it as headquarters during his siege of Istanbul. The church collapsed completely after the conquest of Istanbul.

It was constructed again on the foundations of the old church in 1834 on the

initiative of Patriarch Constantine I and the firman of Mahmut II (1808-1839). The construction of the church was completed in 1835 and it was opened for worship. The church, which was built in an east-west orientation, has a basilical plan and three naves. The narthex situated in the west is oriented north to south and rectangular planned. The ceiling of the five-sectioned narthex is composed of cross shaped vaults. There are six lines of columns between each of the naves. All of these three naves are barrel vaulted.

There is a marble iconostasis comprising three naves at the east of the main floor. The ambon sits on the fifth col-

umn from the front of the northern column series and the despot throne is in front of the third column series from the front of the southern column series. The part of the apse situated in the middle nave axis is semi-rounded eastwards on the inside and it bulges outwards. The gallery appears above the entrance of the main floor. The narthex is rectangular planned in a north-south orientation. The apse has semi conical roof within the structure with a double-faced ribbed roof. The belfry, of iron construction, appears on the roof of the church and also in the south western corner of the church. There are marble gravestones with engravings in the Karaman language on the ground of the court of the church.

ΜΡ ΘΥ
Η ΓΑΛΑΚΤΟΤΡΟΦΟΥΣΑ
Ο Ω Ν

CHURCHES of the GOLDEN HORN

20 KARIYE
KHORA MONASTERY CHURCH

Exterior view of Khora

Kariye, situated inside the ramparts of Istanbul, in Edirnekapi quarter, comes from the word "Khora" meaning out of the city, or rural place, in ancient Greek. Although its exact construction date is not known, it is known that there was previously a chapel here. Kariye church was constructed along with the monastery in about 536 during the reign of the emperor Justinian I (527-565). The church, damaged in the iconoclastic period (724-843), was restored at different times. The removal of the imperial dynasty to Blachernae Palace in the reign of the Comnenus dynasty (1081-1185), and the performance of some religious ceremonies in Kariye church, which was reserved only for the Palace, increased the importance of the church. As a result of this, Maria Doucina, mother-in-law of the emperor Alexius I (1081-1118), took the church under her wings and had it constructed again. The church was pillaged and witnessed great destruction during the Latin invasion (1204-1261). The church went through its most glorious period at the time of the emperor Andronicus II Palaeologus (1282-1328). Theodoro Metochites, a great statesman, politician, man of letters, and scholar in this period, had the church restored extensively. A gallery to the northern wing of

General view of the main floor.

View of the parecclesion.

the church which consists of narthex and main floor, the paracclesion, a chapel with a single narrow and long nave adjacent to southern face, and an outer narthex running along the western face, were added. Also, the mosaic ornamenting the interior and exterior narthexes, and the frescos decorating the paracclesion were done in this period. The high-tamboured and windowed dome sits on four arches above the main floor, which ends with a semi rounded apse at the eastern end. The ground has marble flooring and the walls are coated with marble plates. The marble plates covering the walls are as precious as mosaic decorations because they are both old and figured. The richest mosaic and frescos of the latest golden age of the Byzantine Empire appear in Kariye. The lives of the Virgin Mary and Jesus are illustrated in mosaics that decorate the wall, the arch, the vault, and the domes on the interior and exterior narthexes. On the northern wing of the interior narthex, the life history of the Virgin Mary, on the northern wing of the exterior narthex, important events of the Sacred Family, the birth and the baptism of Jesus are depicted. The marvels and the works of Jesus appear on the southern wings of both narthexes. Some

Image of the Madonna and Child on the dome of the interior narthex.

Image of the Madonna and Child with twelve angels on the parecclesion dome.

subjects from the Torah, to which great importance is given by Christianity, were illustrated on the frescos that decorate the parecclesion.

At the entrance to the exterior narthex, the miracles of the Kana wedding are illustrated on the vault, reciprocally to Jesus Pantocrator and the Virgin Mary between two angels on two doors in its middle part. There are illustrations of the departure to Bethlehem, the census, the birth of Jesus, arrival in Nazareth, and departure to Jerusalem on the northern wing of the exterior narthex, and the early adulthood of Jesus and John the Baptist, Jesus and the Devil, as well as illustrations of Saint Andronicus and Saint Tarchus reciprocally on the vaults. Opposite are illustrations of King Herod and the diviners, the inquisition of Herod, the order of child massacre, the lament of the mothers, Elisabeth and John, and the massacre of children, on the southern wing of the exterior narthex, the rehabilitation of the leper and the rehabilitation of the paralysed, and Samarian woman on the vaults.

The scenes of Jesus and Theodoro Metochites, and the Virgin Mary taking wood from the temple, appear reciprocally on two doors in the middle of the interior narthex, with the introduction of

Angel image on the parecclesion dome.

Image of Saint Tarchus.

Detail from the scene of Anastasis (Resurrection) in the parecclesion apse.

the Virgin Mary to the temple engraved on the vault. The illustrations of the refusal of presentations, Joachim in desert, the scene of the gospel, the meeting of Joachim and Anna, the birth of the Virgin Mary, the first steps of the Virgin Mary, Zechariah and the twelve staffs, the conception of Jesus to the Virgin Mary, the carriage of the Virgin Mary to home, the scene of the gospel, the adieu of Joseph

Image of Jesus curing a paralysed man in the upper portion of the panel, while in the lower portion are scenes of King Herod's order of child massacre

to the Virgin Mary, and Saint Peter are engraved on the left wing of the interior narthex. And the scenes of the caress of the Virgin Mary by her mother and father and the sanctification of the Virgin Mary are engraved on the vault. Figures of the Virgin Mary and child Jesus are depicted in the middle of the dome, and the ancestors of Jesus are depicted on the segments of the dome. The figures of

Image of the Madonna and Child with twelve angels on the parecclesion dome.

Image of Saint Petros.

Image of the Virgin Mary of Hodegetria on the main floor

the sixteen prophet kings; David, Solomon, Rehaboam, Abia, Asa, Jehosaphat, Joram, Ozias, Joatham, Achaz, Ezekiel, Manasseh, Amon, Josiah, Jechoniah, and Salathiel respectively are depicted on the upper part of the segments of the dome, and the figures of Hananiah, Azariah, Mishael, Daniel, Joshua, Moses, Aaron, Hur, Samuel, Job, and Melchizedek are illustrated on the lower part. On the right wing of the interior narthex, the scenes of Saint Paul, the nourishment of the Virgin Mary, the cure of two blind men, the cure of a crowd of people, the cure of the blind and the dumb, the cure of the leper, the cure of a juvenile whose arm is diseased, the woman seeking healing, Jesus of Khalke, and the healing of the mother-in-law of Peter are depicted. Jesus Pantocrator is illustrated in the middle of the dome; the figures of 24 ancestors of Jesus in two lines on the segments of the dome are represented. On the upper part of the segments of the dome, the figures of Adam, Seth, Noah, Cainan, Maleleel, Jared, Lamech, Sem, Japheth, Aiphaxad, Sala, Heber, Saruch, Nachor, Thara, Abraham, Isaac, Jacob, Phalec, Ragau,

Mosaic image of Jesus Pantocrator above the door leading to the interior narthex.

Detail from the scene of Anastasis (Resurrection) on the semi-dome of the parecclesion apse.

Methuselah, Enoch, Enos and Abel are portrayed; the figures of the twelve sons of Yakub, two sons of Judah and one son of Phares appear on the lower part of the segments of the dome. These are Reuben, Simeon, Levi, Judah, Zebulun, Issachar, Dam, Gad, Asher, Naphtali, Joseph, Benjamin, Pharez, Zarah and Esrom respectively.

There are images of the death of the Vir-

gin Mary above the entrance gate (inside) of the main floor, Jesus standing holding the Bible on the front facade of the northern rank of the apse, The Virgin Mary standing with the child Jesus in her arms (the Virgin Mary of Hodogetria) on the front facade of the southern rank of the apse.

The walls and the ceiling of the Parecclesion are ornamented with frescos, which

Mosaic image of Jesus and his forefathers on the dome, and of the Madonna and Child on the arch

include scenes taken from the Bible and the Torah. The depicted scenes include; Anastasis (Resurrection) on the dome of apse, illustrations of Saint Athanasius, Saint John Chrysostom, Saint Basil, Theologian Saint Gregory and Alexandrian Saint Cyril on the wall of the apse, images of archangel Michael, the resurrection of the daughter of Jairus, the resurrection of the son of the widowed woman and the Virgin Mary of Eleousa on the arch in front of the apse, the scene of the last hearing (Deesis) and the image of the angel who carries heaven on the ceiling in front of the arch, the scenes of Abraham and Lazarus, the rich man in hell, the Angel and child, Angels and the dead, the people in hell, the bearers of the Ark of Covenant, people going to heaven, and the Virgin Mary and child Jesus on the lateral walls.

In the domed section of the Parecclesion, there are illustrations of the Virgin Mary and Child Jesus in a medallion in the middle of the dome, and illustrations of twelve angels on the segments of the dome. The illustrations of Saint Jean Damascene, Saint Cosmos, Saint Joseph, and Saint Theophane, four poet Bible-writers appear on the pendentives of the dome. Scenes from the dream of Yakup, Moses in the bush, Solomon and the nation of Israel, and the placement of the Ark of Covenant

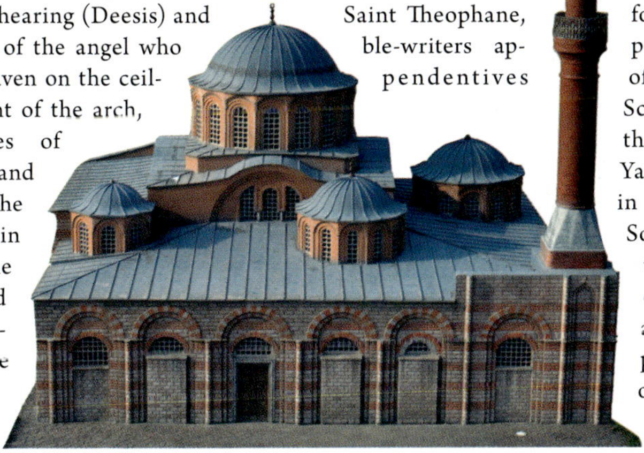

Kariye in the Miniature Museum of Miniaturk İstanbul

Mosaic image of Jesus seated on a throne with Theodoro Metochites

are depicted on the lateral walls of this section. The tomb in the niche on the southern wall of this domed section belongs to Saint Michael Tornikes and his wife Eugenia. On the arch that follows the domed section, scenes of the war with the Assyrians in front of Jerusalem, and Aaron and his children in the Temple, are depicted. Also, heroic soldier images appear on the walls of the Parecclesion.

The scene of the Ascension of the Virgin Mary (Koimesis), which appears above the door in the main floor, particularly moves spectators. The scenes of the Resurrection (Anastasis) and Last Judgement (Deesis) in the Parecclesion attract attention with their dimensions. The scene of the Resurrection (Anastasis) is unquestionably a masterpiece of Christian art with its magnificence and ani-

mation. Also, the niches that appear on the interior walls of the interior and exterior narthexes, and the Parecclesion were used as tombs for famous persons.
After the conquest of Istanbul in 1453 by Turks, the church of Kariye continued its function for a while, but was converted to a mosque in 1511 by Hadım Ali Pasha, the Grand Vizier of Sultan Bayezit II (1481-1512). The minaret was added to the southern end of the exterior narthex. Mosaics and frescos were left untouched. They were only covered by plaster and wooden shutters. Kariye was converted to a museum in 1945. The building underwent extensive restoration between the years 1948 and 1958 and all mosaics and frescos were cleaned and revealed.

Scene of the Ascension of the Virgin Mary (Koimesis) in the main floor

Detail from the scene of Anastasis (Resurrection) in the parecclesion apse

21 MOSQUE OF FETHİYE PAMMAKARITOS MONASTRY CHURCH

Exterior view of Fethiye Mosque

Pammakaristos church situated in Çarşamba quarter of Fatih district, dedicated to the Virgin Mary was built by Mihail Glabas Tarkaniotes, one of the leading personalities of the Byzantine Palace at the end of the 13th century (1294). Maria Doucina had the Parecclesion building constructed in 1355 next to the church at the southeast end in memory of her husband Mihail Glabas Tarkaniotes.

The paracclesion, which is an important part of the church, was built according to a cross plan with four columns. Two windowed domes cover the narthex and the main floor has a tambour-framed dome with twelve windows. Its main dome has twelve segments, with mosaic images of Jesus in the middle, and mosaic illustrations of prophets of the Torah appear in the segments. There are mosaics containing the scene of Deesis (Day of Armageddon), which include Jesus, the Virgin Mary, and John in the apse section. Moreover, there are mosaics and frescos that include saint images on the vaults and the arches.

After its conversion to a mosque, great changes were made inside the building. The apse section was pulled down and a domed area was added including an al-

General view of the parecclesion ceiling

Image of Jesus on the dome of the apse

tar in the direction of Mecca, and also the columns between the ranks were removed and the weight of the dome was loaded onto two arches, constructed in opposition. Besides, a minaret was added to the corner of the building. Grand Vizier Mustafa Pasha had a madrasah (Muslim theological school) constructed to the western end of it.

An external gallery that surrounds these

Images of Jesus and the twelve Old Testament Prophets on the parecclesion dome

Images of saints

Images of saints

two adjacent structures on three sides was added in the subsequent period. A dome that sits on windowed tambours covers the main floor in the main original church supported by four ranks. The structure, having been used as a women's monastery after the conquest of Istanbul, was used as Greek Patriarchate for 150 years beginning from the year 1455. At the end of the 16th century (1590), it was converted to a mosque by Ahmet Pasha and called "Fethiye Mosque" in commemoration of the conquest of Azerbaijan and Georgia. The mosque was damaged in the Balatkapı fire in 1640. According to the epigraph that appears on the southern gate of the mosque, it was restored in 1845. The mosque, largely restored between the years 1936 and 1938 was only opened to prayer in the 1960s. In the same years, the restoration of the Parecclesion, which is the cemetery chapel of the church, was performed, and all of the mosaics and frescos were revealed by the American Byzantine Institute. The Pareccle-sion section is today open to visitors under the name of "Museum of Fethiye".

General view of Fethiye

General view from the parecclesion

22 HOLY SPRING OF BLACHERNAE

The holy spring situated at the location where Bahçe Kapısı Kuyu Street, Mustafa Paşa Bostan Street and Dervişzade Street intersect, and which belongs to the Byzantine period was dedicated to the Virgin Mary. Empress Pulcheria had Panayia Blachernae Church constructed to a basilical plan with three naves in Ayvansaray during the reign of Emperor Marcian (450-457). But there is nothing left of this church today. The holy spring of Blachernae was constructed in 473, next to the Church of Panayia Blachernae during the reign of Emperor Leo I (457-474).

The holy spring was restored in the reign of emperor Justinian I (527-565). The holy spring and Waterway were renewed in the reign of Emperor Basil II (976-1025). It was damaged by fire in 1069 during the reign of Emperor Romanus Diogenes IV (1068-1071) and was immediately restored. The holy spring also takes its part in the pillage during the Latin invasion in 1204. It was damaged by fire in 1434 and spent the Ottoman era in a ruined state. The stone church building of today

was constructed in the middle of the 19th century in place of the church of Panayia Blachernae. The structure of the holy spring was brought to its current condition. The water of the holy spring comes from the direction of Eğri Kapi. The holy spring adjoins the right hand side of the iconostasis at the southern end of the church, and is a structure with no significant architectural characteristics. An icon on the interior wall of the holy spring depicts a composition of "the Virgin Mary of Hodegetria" consisting of the Virgin Mary with the child Jesus in her arms. The image of a two-headed eagle ap-

pears in the middle of the front arch. The holy spring was frequently visited by the body public during the Byzantine period because of the feast commencing on the July 2nd. Moreover, it is known that the emperors also came here to dip three times into the holy pool, where the water that flows from the hand of the relief of the Virgin Mary is gathered. Today, the holy spring is

in extremely good repair. Although it is visited by the orthodox community of Istanbul and foreign guests, the number of visitors to the holy spring, and the number of the religious community of the church, have steadily decreased in recent years. There is another holy spring dedicated to Saint Katerina at the western side of the church, in a different place.

23 MOSQUE OF ATİK MUSTAFA PASHA
Prophet/Hazreti Cabir

The structure that is called Mosque of Cabir, with the belief that the tomb of Prophet Cabir is inside, is a Byzantine church situated in Ayvansaray quarter of Fatih district. The old name of the church couldn't be determined. However, according to the specialists, this structure would most probably be the church of Aya Tekla. The condition of the church during the conquest of Istanbul is also not exactly known.

The church was converted to a mosque by Koca Mustafa Pasha, one of the Grand Viziers of Yavuz Sultan Selim (1512-1520). The building was greatly damaged in the earthquake of 1509 and the fires which happened in 1729. Its minaret, which collapsed in the earthquake of 1509, was reconstructed. The restorations continued until the year 1906.

The cell at the right hand side of the apse was made in the shape of a tomb and is known as the tomb of Prophet Cabir. The church fits into the closed cross planned group. Its main floor, with four supporting columns, must have been cov-

ered by a windowed dome with tambour frame. But, its current dome with oblate tambour and without windows was built in the restoration resulting from the earthquake of 1509. The narthex of the church is not present at the entrance where it should be. In its place, there is a simple final congregation area with no significant architectural characteristics whose date of construction is not known. There are no ornaments of the Byzantine period inside the building. The wooden pulpit and marble sermon pulpit belonging to the ottoman era also have no artistic characteristics. The fountain of the mosque is situated across the street passing in front of it. There is a drinking fountain constructed by Şatır Hasan Agha in 1692 next to the fountain.

24 CHURCH OF TAKSIARHES

It is on the street of Ayan that descends to Golden Horn in Balat quarter, Fatih district. The church, situated in a large court surrounded by high walls and houses is also called "Ayia Strati". The Greek Private School of Balat and the holy spring of Mihaiş, which are not used today, are located at the northern end of the court. The holy spring of Ayios Nikolaos at the eastern end and the belfry at the northern end are adjacent to the church. It is known that the church, mentioned in the lists of Tryphon dated 1583 and Paterakis dated 1604 respectively, was badly damaged in the fire of Balat in 1730. According to the epigraph of the church, it was restored in 1833 during the reign of Patriarch Constantine I.

The church is built to a rectangular plan. The apse makes a semi round protrusion eastwards. The structure is covered with two-faced ribbed roofs. However, the cover of the apse is a semi conical roof. The wooden narthex at the western end was added to the building later on and is built to a rectangular plan in a north-south orientation. The church, built in a basilical plan, has three naves. Westwards, there are three entrances to the main floor from the line of naves.

There are six lines of columns, connected to each other by architrave, between each of the naves. There is a semi-rounded apse at the eastern end in line with the middle nave. The altar is in the middle of the apse. The interior cover of the apse is a semi dome. There are three niches of equal length at the northern side of the apse. There is a smaller niche at the southern side. The dais part is a step higher than the naves. The gallery, which sits on the last columns in the west of the main floor, protrudes towards the lateral

naves. Ascent to the gallery is provided by wooden stairs inside the belfry in the north. The middle nave is covered by low vault and the lateral naves are covered by flat ceiling in the wooden cover system of the church.

The wooden iconostasis, which includes the eastward three naves, the wooden ambon that sits on the fourth column from the front of the northern column line, and the despot throne, next to the second line from the front of the southern column line, are ornamented with herbal, geometric motifs in relief and sculpture technique.

25 HREŞDAGABET (SURP) CHURCH

The history of the church situated at Kamış Street in Balat quarter in Fatih district dates back earlier than the 17th century. Although it was a Greek church previously, the church was given to Armenians in about 1627, after the Greeks left the church in the 17th century. According to its epigraph, the church, whose restoration was completed in 1628, was opened for worship.

However, the church witnessed several fires. The first fire happened after the opening of the church for worship in the same year. The church whose restoration was completed in a short time opened again for worship. The church was largely damaged in the fire of 1692 and was ruined in the fire of 1729. It underwent great restoration and was opened again to prayer. Because the wooden church aged in the course of time, it was pulled down from the base and constructed again. The construction of the church was completed in 1835 and opened for worship. Although it has seen some restoration in the second half of the 20th century, the building stands in its original state nowadays.

It is a group of structures rather than a church. There are chapels and a holy spring beside

the main church. There is a large narthex at the entrance of the church, constructed in an east-west axis and to a basilical plan. The narthex is divided into three by two columns. The lateral sections are one step higher than the middle section. The cover of the narthex is flat. There is a gallery allocated to the choir above the narthex. One passes through an iron-framed structure after the narthex to the main floor, which has three naves. There is a line of columns between the naves. The columns are connected to each other by arches. The main floor, lateral naves, and the gallery are covered by cradle vault. The next area, separated from the

naves by wooden barriers, is allocated to the choir and the clergymen. The door that opens northwards from this section goes to the baptistery chapel dedicated to Surp Boğos (Saint Pavlus) and Surp Bedros (Saint Petros), however, the door that opens to the south goes to the chapel of Surp Lısavori. It is followed by the altar area to which one ascends via three steps. The church has three bigger apses in the middle part. The apses are jagged outside

and semi-rounded inside, and are covered by semi domes. The altar in the middle apse was dedicated to Saint Archangel Gabriel, the altar in the northern apse to Çarkhapan Surp Asdvadzadzin, and the altar in the southern apse to Surp Minas. Although the chapel of Lusavoriç at the south of the church consists of just one gallery, the Baptistery Chapel that is dedicated to Surp Boğos and Bedros at the north is a chapel of a basilical plan. There

is an altar that is said to belong to Khintragadar Surp Azdvadzadzin at the right hand side of the exit of this chapel. One arrives at the holy spring of the chapel of Surp Ardem (Saint/Priestess Ardemos) situated in the basement through stairs on the left hand side of this altar. The historical, two-winged iron door at the north western side of the main floor is completely ornamented with pictures. In these pictures, the scene in which Jesus drives the sellers away from a temple in Jerusalem by scourge is depicted. Also, the inside of the church is ornamented with old pictures.

26 CHURCH OF PANAYIA MUHLIOTISSA

It is located between Firketeci Street and Tevkii Cafer School Street in Fener quarter of Fatih district. It was dedicated to the Virgin Mary. It is also known as the Mongolian Church. The church appears at the north eastern end of a small court with high walls. The holy spring of Ayia Anna is situated at the south western end of the court. The history of the church, which is thought to be situated in the place of an old monastery, dates back to the 10th century. It is said that the church was constructed in the 11th century. The possession of the monastery, at which was found the church that belongs to Maria Akropolitissa until the 12th century, passed to Maria Palaeologus, the daughter of Emperor Michael VIII (1259-1282) at this time. The church, constructed in 1261, after the Latin invasion, was damaged by fire in1633, 1640 and 1729; its architecture was changed and lost its originality due to the restoration that was carried out. Having been constructed before the conquest of Istanbul, the church is unique in that it was not converted to a mosque after the conquest of Istanbul, and continues its function as a place of Greek orthodox worship even today. Besides, it is the only example of the Byzantine churches built to a four-leafed clover plan in Istanbul still standing.

The church is built to a plan covered by a dome and four semi-domes in the centre. The narthex section was added in the 14th century. The only entrance to the main floor is from the narthex. The narthex is covered with cross vaults. There are symmetrical

niches on the apse. The gallery is situated above the narthex. The structure underwent changes in restorations made in different periods. The dome of the church, covered by a ribbed roof on the outside, is a simple dome with a cylindrical tambour, sitting on an octagonal base at the northeast end of the church and is conically framed. There is a belfry of baldachin shape made of brick materials in the southwest corner of the church.

The wood iconostasis at the east of the main floor, the despot throne at the southern side, and the wood ambon at the southeast are ornamented with herbal motives of sculpture and relief technique. The icons on the lower line of the iconostasis are dated 1884 and are coated with silver in relief technique.

27 GREEK PATRIARCHATE OF FENER
YEORYİOS (AYIOS) PATRIARCHATE CHURCH

Christianity was accepted as a religion during the time of the Emperor Constantine I (324-337). At the end of the council meeting held in İznik in 325, all suppression was removed. The construction of churches as places of belief commenced. Orthodox is one of the three grand Christian centres. It means "eastern blood" in Greek. They object especially to the Papal institution and accept Jesus as unique authority of Christianity (power-authority). Istanbul, which became the capital of the Byzantine Empire in 330, had been an important centre of religious discussion in the Christian World beginning in the 6th century. The church of the Eastern Roman Empire (Byzantine Empire), which complied with the decisions taken at seven council meetings, held between 325 and 787, and which didn't recognize subsequent decisions, were the founders of the orthodox cult. Once the orthodox churches that didn't recognize the papacy and were separated from Rome in 1054 were divided into two parts, East and West, the Patriarchate of Fener, in Fener in Istanbul became the centre of the Eastern Church. After the conquest of Istanbul in 1453, the Greek Patriarchate of Fener was founded by permission of Fatih Sultan Mehmet. The first patriarch Gennadios II conducted his work in the church of Havariyum,

constructed in the reign of Emperor Constantine I, and is the second biggest church in the city. Upon the construction of Fatih Mosque in place of this church, the patriarchate was moved to the Monastery of Panmakaristos in 1455. When this monastery was converted to a mosque in 1586, the patriarchate, which was first moved to the Church of Vlah (Eflak) Palace in Fener, and then to the Church of Hagios Demetrios in 1597 in Ayvansaray, was moved to the monastery of Hagios Georgios in Fener in 1602 and it continues its services there. The authority given to the patriarchate by firman of Fatih was

used by patriarchs. The duties of the patriarchs were re-determined by the administrative reforms of 1839, a series of reforms undertaken in the Ottoman Empire to modernize society along secular and bureaucratic lines. The patriarchate was limited to being a religious institution by the Treaty of Lausanne of 1924. After the proclamation

of the republic, the Patriarchate of the Greek Orthodox took its place as an independent church within the rules of the secular state. A fire broke out in the service building of the Patriarchate in 1941. The restoration works that were started in 1989 were completed in 1991. Today, the Patriarchate continues its work in this building.

It is situated in the northern part of a court surrounded by high walls located between Grand Vizier Ali Pahsa Street and Incebel Street in Fener quarter in Fatih district. Also there are; the holy spring of Ayios Haralambos, the library and administrative buildings in the court along with the Patriarchate of the Greek Orthodox. The place adjoining the southwest end of the church is the place where sacred "myrrh" oil, used for liturgical purposes by Greek Orthodox Churches is produced.

S. Gerlach, who conveys information about the church in his note dated May 15th, 1578, features the church as "Tower Church". Patriarch Timothy II had the new church constructed in 1614. The church, introduced as Patriarchate Church by Kömürciyan in the second half of the 17th century, was enlarged in 1698, in the reign of Patriarch Kallinikos II. According to the epigraph dated December 18th, 1720 the church was rebuilt in the reign of Patriarch Ieremias III. Inciyan describes the structure, which he characterizes as Patriarchate Church at the end of the 18th century, as the Church of Aya Yorgi, surrounded by ramparts at the foot of the

fifth hill in Fener. Patriarch Gregory V was hung at the entrance gate of the Patriarchate in 1821 for affiliating with the Greek rebellion. The church underwent restoration in 1827. Again according to its epigraph, the church was rebuilt during the reign of the Patriarch Gregory VI in 1836. The church, renewed after the fire of 1941, is today used as the Patriarchate Church.

Three symmetrical apses, one in the middle and two at the sides protrude eastwards of the church, which has an irregular rectangular plan in an east-west

orientation. The apses in the middle and in the south have a semi-rounded plan externally, and the apse in the north has a rectangular plan akin to a square externally. The middle nave is covered by double-faced, refracted framed roofs; however the lateral naves are covered with single-faced roofs. The cover of the northern apse is a single-faced roof; the cover of the other two apses is semi-conical. The church has a basilical plan type. The main floor, with three naves, is bounded by three apses at the eastern end. There are seven lines of columns between the naves. The middle nave is barrel vaulted; the lateral naves are flat ceilinged. The narthex is built to a rectangular plan and the two-floored gallery situated above it extends towards the main floor over the lateral naves. Three doors open from the narthex to the main floor in line with the naves.

The middle one of these doors has an arch and the lateral ones are rectangular shaped. The wooden iconostasis comprising three naves at the east of the main floor, the wooden ambon that sits on the fifth column from the front of the column series at the north end, and the wooden patriarch throne situated next to the second column from the front of the column series at the southern end, are

ornamented with herbal and geometric motifs in sculpture and relief technique.

The fact that the Patriarchate is located here increased the historical and religious importance of the church. Different materials that were considered sacred to Christianity are gathered here. The stone believed to be the column at which Jesus was tied and whipped, is in the southern part of the iconostasis. Again in front of the iconostasis, at the south eastern end of the main floor, there are three coffins in which are the relics of Saint/Priestess Eufemia and her two followers, and mosaic icons. It is said that the throne of the patriarch dates back to the 5th century.

28 BULGARIAN CHURCH OF STEPHAN (SVETI)

Bulgarian citizens living within the territories of the Ottoman State were worshipping in orthodox churches bound to the Patriarchate of the Greek Orthodox at Fener. In the 19th century they attempt to establish their own independent church, and they succeeded. First, they thought of constructing a church on the shore of the Golden Horn. However, they decided not to construct it due to the fact that the foundation of a masonry construction would subside, because the soil base on the shore of the Golden Horn is not strong, so they started the project by choosing an iron framework to make it lighter. They had the plan of the construction prepared for Hovsep Aznavur, Armenian architect from Istanbul.

Stevi Stephan Church is situated be-

tween the districts of Balat and Fener on the shore of the Golden Horn. The entire structure was prefabricated and made of iron materials. The Austrian company R.Ph. Waagner, which won the contract to construct the church in 1892, commenced production in 1893. After all components were completed, they were transported to Istanbul from Vienna, via the River Danube and the Black Sea, erected in situ and opened for worship in 1898.

The church was constructed on a basement which rises a bit from ground level. Besides the main entrance at the south western end, it has two additional doors on both lateral facades. One enters from the narthex to the main floor by three doors located in line with the naves. The door that opens to the middle nave has an iron frame. The section in which prayer is performed is separated from the apse by a gilded wood iconostasis. There is a "U" shaped gallery above the two lateral naves and the entrance section. The gallery is covered by cross vault and the middle nave and the transept are covered by cylindrical barrel vault. The main floor was kept higher than the naves. The narthex and the gallery have a flat ceiling. The upper section of the gallery entrance belongs to the choir. There is a belfry above the choir section. One ascends to the belfry by a spiral staircase in the corner. The exterior facades of the structure are extremely ornamented. The structure, which consists of new gothic and new baroque elements in terms of style, was shaped with an eclectic conception.

29 GÜL/ROSE MOSQUE

Theodosia (Ayia) Church

The exact date of construction of the church located in Ayakapi quarter on the shore of the Golden Horn is not known. It is said that the church was constructed on behalf of Saint/Priestess Eufemia and was converted to Theodosia later on. The church, built in the reign of Emperor Basil I (867-886), or formed by the restoration of an old structure, is a religious structure and has also been a cemetery church. The tombs of some personages of the Imperial dynasty are here.

Because the woman named Theodosia, who was killed resisting those attempting to bring down the icon of Jesus on the Khalke Door, which opens to the Great Palace from Hagia Sophia Circus, became Christian later on, her cadaver and sacred belongings were put into this church in the iconoclastic period (724-843). The church underwent huge restoration in the 13th century after the Latin invasion (1204-1261).

According to rumour, the church was ornamented with roses on May 29th, 1453, the holyday of priestesses. The Turks, entering the city on the conquest of Istanbul, saw the church ornamented with roses, and called it Rose Mosque when it was converted to a mosque. According to another rumour, it took its name from Gülbaba whose tomb is situated in a dais on the right hand side of the altar.

The church was used a depot for ship equipment after the conquest of Istanbul. However, it was converted to a

mosque by Hasan Pasha during the reign of Sultan Selim II (1566-1574). The structure was largely restored during the reign of Mahmut II (1808-1839). The restorations of the Ottoman era, which were made not only on the big supporting arches but also on the main dome, are clearly seen.

The main building was constructed over a basement with brick vault. The structure is built to a plan of a closed Greek cross with four grades. There are three apses at the eastern end, the middle one very large. The galleries on three sides each sit on two ranks. The galleries are two floored. One ascends to the gallery from the left hand side of the narthex. The wooden Sultan's Pew appears at the eastern end in the northward part of the second floor gallery. The structure lost its originality largely as a result of interventions made during the Ottoman era and it almost became a work of Ottoman art. There is a minaret that was constructed from stone after the earthquake of 1766 in the southwest corner of the structure.

30 OLD IMARET MOSQUE
Pantepoptes Monastery Church

It is situated on a steep slope going down to the Golden Horn from Fatih. A gallery equal in size to the structure was built under the building. This gallery was used as a reservoir later on. Pantepoptes Monastery Church was dedicated to "all seeing" Jesus. The monastery must have been constructed by Anna Comnenus, the mother of the emperor Alexius Comnenus (1081-1118), between the years 1081-1087 during the Byzantine period. While the monastery was being converted to an imaret, small dervish lodge, and madrasah, the church was used as a mosque, dormitory, final congregation area, soup kitchen and dining hall for the students of a special Koran course. The structure was largely restored in the 1970s. The wooden altar and pulpit in the mosque have no artistic characteristics.

It is the most distinctive example of four-columned closed cross-planned churches in Istanbul. The church, with a cross vault at the western end, was constructed in an east-west orientation and has two narthexes, exterior and interior. There is a gallery above the interior narthex. Three doors open to the main floor from the interior narthex. The main floor, built to a closed-cross plan, has four supporters and is covered by a windowed dome with high tambour frame. There is one four leafed clover-shaped cell at each of the two sides of the apse. The dome of the apse is covered by tiles.

31 ZEYREK MOSQUE

Pantokrator Monastery Church

When Pantocrator Monastery Church situated in Ibadethane Street in Zeyrek quarter of Fatih district was converted to a madrasah after the conquest of Istanbul, this quarter was called Zeyrek quarter after Zeyrek Mehmet Efendi, the first professor of the madrasah.

The construction of the church was started by Eirene, the daughter of the emperor John Comnenus (118-1143), and was completed in 1136 by his father, Emperor John II when Eirene died. The church was dedicated to Jesus Pantocrator, the sovereign of the universe. However, a church dedicated to the Virgin Mary to the north of this big church before the year 1136, and a tomb chapel dedicated to Archangel Michael between these two churches, were constructed. Therefore, it became a triple structure. The architect of the church and the monastery was a master workman named Nicephorus. The monastery and the church underwent restoration after the Latin invasion (1204-1261).

The Empress Eirene, who died in 1124, and the Emperor John II, who died in

1143, were buried in the tomb situated here. The tomb of Bertha von Sulzbach, wife of Manuel I, who died in 1158, the tomb of Eirene, wife of Emperor Andronicus II (1282-1328), the tombs of Manuel II (1391-1425) who died in 1425 and his brother Andronicus who died in 1426, the tomb of Maria the princess of Trabzon who died in 1439, the tomb of Eugenia, wife of John VII (1390), who died in 1440, the tomb of Manuel and John VIII (1425-1448) who died in 1448, and the tomb of Eirene, wife of Manuel Palaeologus (1391-1425), who died in 1450 were in Pantocrator Monastery. The relics and sacred bequests of some Saints were protected in Pantocrator Monastery. Also, it was believed that the wooden tripod on which Jesus was laid after being brought down from the crucifix was also here.

The oldest structure of the Pantocrator Monastery Church complex, which consists of three buildings, is the big church dedicated to Jesus Pantocrator. There is a five-sectioned narthex constructed in later periods, which belongs to this church. The middle part of the narthex is covered with a dome that has a high barrel vault. The southern church includes a closed Greek cross-shaped plan with four columns. The apse of the

church, comprising windows and niches, protrudes. The church dedicated to the Virgin Mary is a smaller example of the southern church in terms of plan. The main dome was set on four ranks that are square-sectioned. The exterior part of the narthex section was largely restored. The tomb chapel located between both churches is covered with two oval shaped domes. The chapel has a narrow and long area.

The three churches of the Pantocrator Monastery were converted to madrasah after the conquest of Istanbul. The name of Zeyrek Mosque was given to the structure, which was converted to a mosque following completion of the construction of the madrasah in the Islamic-ottoman social complex of Istanbul. Also, it is known as Mullah Zeyrek Mosque. The mosque's altar and mess of the Sultan, largely restored in 18th century, were remade in baroque style in this century. Its minaret has been recently renewed.

CHURCHES of BEYOĞLU-ŞİŞLİ

32 TRIAS (AYIA) CHURCH

It is situated in a square surrounded by Taksim, Sıraselviler, Istiklal Street and Meşelik Street in Beyoğlu quarter. The church, which is in a large garden, is a domed masonry structure built to a cross plan. According to the epigraph on the door situated on the right hand side of the narthex, the church was built in 1880. The architect of the structure is Vasilaki Ioannidi Effendi.

One enters the narthex of the church by ascending the marble stairs at the western end. There are three doors, one of which is in the direction of the main floor, and the others are to the north and south. The main dome of the church was set on a high tambour frame on top of arches connecting four supporters. There is an image of Jesus Pantocrator in the middle of the tambour frame of the dome, and images of angels on its pendentives. As well as these, there are twelve windows on the tambour frame of the dome with images of saints between them.

The floor of the church is marbled. The galleries, situated above the narthexes and the naves, are cross-vaulted. There are icons on the facades of the galleries

that look out on the main floor, located at both sides of the main floor. These galleries sit on four columns each at both sides. One climbs three steps to the apse. There is an altar in the middle of the cross-vaulted apse. The marble iconostasis, located in the east of the main floor, is ornamented with relief motives and four small columns. The ambon is made of marble and the archpriests' throne is made of marble and onyx. There is a belfry in each of the southern and northern corners on the west side of the church.

ΙΕΖΕΚΙΗΛ
ΣΟΛΟΜΩΝ
ΓΕΔΕΩΝ

33 CHURCH OF SAINT ESPRIT

The church is located in the court of the French Girl's High School of Notre Dame de Sion, situated on Cumhuriyet (Republic) Street in Harbiye quarter of Şişli district. The church was constructed at the same time as the French Girl's High School of Notre Dame de Sion. A second entrance was provided to the basement from Ölçek Street at the back of the structure. The church was constructed in 1846 by Hillereau, who was in Istanbul as a representative of the Pope, and is a masterpiece of the Italian-born Swiss architect Giussepe Fossati. The church was largely damaged by the earthquake of 1865. It was thoroughly renewed by the catholic Greek architect Pietro Vitalis from Istanbul and was put into service in the same year. The statue of Pope Benedict XV, located in the court of the church and the French Girl's High School, was made by sculptor Quattrini in 1921.

The church, constructed in an east-west orientation on sloping land is a rectangular planned Latin basilica with three naves and measures 35x16 meters. The church, whose exterior facades are plastered, is covered with a barrel roof. An additional structure in the shape of a passage was appended to the south of the building. The entrance of the church is on the eastern side. The main floor is bounded at the west by three square-planned apses in line with the naves. The middle apse, where there is a richly ornamented altar, is separated from the flat-ceilinged main floor by a large rounded arch. There is a line of sev-

en columns, with Ionic capital, and a rank between the naves. A wooden ambon sits on the third column from the front of the right-hand column row. The gallery that starts above the eastern entrance, and that sits on the columns, continues over the lateral naves.

The main baroque style entrance, forming the eastern façade of the church, looks out into the court. The belfry rises at the western end of the church. The belfry, with a clock on its façade, represents a simple renaissance style. There are tombs of some important personalities, from old church officials and the congregation of the church, under its basement.

34 THE VIRGIN MARY SYRIAN ORTHODOX KADIM CHURCH

It is situated in Karakum Street in Tarlabaşı, in Beyoğlu district. The proximity of the Armenian and Syrian Churches to each other stems from the fact that both churches are bound to the orthodox group of churches. The Armenian Church had precedence over other orthodox churches at the end of the 5th century and the beginning of the 6th century. The Syrian orthodox, along with other churches, were taking their authorizations and official approvals under the auspices of the Armenians.

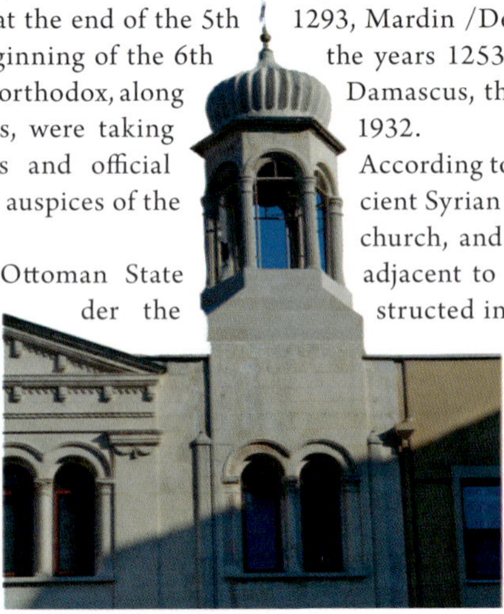

Minorities in the Ottoman State were gathered under the protection of the Greek and Armenian Patriarchates. The Syrian Orthodox, Georgian, Armenian, Alan, Coptic, and Ethiopian minorities, bound to the Monophysite belief, were protected by the Armenian Patriarchate. The religious centre of the Syrian Orthodox Patriarchate had been Antioch up until 518, various places from 518 to 969, Malatya between the years 969 and 1058, Diyarbakır between the years 1058 and 1293, Mardin /Deyrul Zafaran between the years 1253 and 1932, and finally Damascus, the capital of Syria after 1932.

According to the history of the Ancient Syrian Orthodox Church, the church, and metropolitic domicile adjacent to the church, were constructed in 1844. A new church, whose construction expenses were provided by Istepan Agha from Izmir, and is a masterpiece of the architect Serope Kalfa, was constructed in 1863 in place of the

same church. While property of the church was given to the Armenian people, under an agreement made before putting the church into service in the same year, it was decided that Armenian and Syrian people would perform religious services equally in the church. The church, which was badly damaged in the Beyoğlu fire of 1870, underwent extensive restoration in 1878, and was again put into religious service. In place of the structure pulled down in 1961, the building, whose foundation was laid by Syrian Patriarch Yakub (Jacob) III, and whose construction continued for two years, was opened for worship after completion in 1963. But when, over the course of time, the worship area of the church couldn't meet the need for areas of social activity, as well as life space, a complex that would give services with contemporaneous meaning to all units of the metropolitic was put in place, by means of construction work carried out in the years 2004-2006 after pulling down all the buildings around the church in 2003.

The church was constructed in a basilical style. One enters the main floor, separated for worship, through three doors at the northern end and two doors at the southern end. There are ranks adjacent to the two walls at the east and west sides of the main floor. There is a "U"-shaped gallery supported by two columns at the west end of the main floor. The apse appears at the eastern end of the main floor. The apse has a door at each of the north and south ends. There is an altar in the semi-rounded niche of the apse.

All the exterior facades of the church are simple structures, the belfry, the altar inside, the capitals, and some parts were brought specially from Mardin and were graved by the masters from Mardin living in Istanbul, and ornamented with cream-coloured stones. The arched door ornamented with rose motifs at the entrance of the church, all of the arched windows, the belfry and the reliefs of angel and cross on the triangle pediment of the church give richness to the structure.

35 CONSTANTINE (AYIOS) ELENI (AYIA) CHURCH

It is situated in the middle of a court surrounded by high walls and Kalyoncu Kulluğu Street and Kemerbostanı Street in Beyoğlu district. According to its epigraph, Patriarch Joachim II had it constructed between the years 1856 and 1861. The church, built in a north-south orientation has a rectangular plan. The cover of the roof protrudes northwards and southwards until the line of the dome. There are three semi-rounded apses in the eastern axis, and two belfries extending from the north and south corners. There is an altar in the middle of the main apse. The main floor has three naves. The middle nave and the apse are barrel-vaulted and the galleries are cross-vaulted. The church is bounded by three apses at the eastern end in line with the naves, and by a rectangular planned narthex in a north-south orientation at the west. The "U"-shaped gallery, placed above the narthex, reaches over the main floor above the two lateral naves. The area belonging to the choir and the spirituals is one step higher, and the apse is three steps higher, than the main floor.

The main floor, determined by four cross ranks, protrudes to the north and south. The main floor is domed, on a tambour frame with pendentives, while the projections at the sides are low vault. One enters

the main floor from the narthex through three doors in line with the naves. The middle door is arched and the lateral ones are rectangular. One ascends to the belfries through the doors at the north and south ends of the narthex, which is cross-vaulted.

There are illustrations of Jesus Pantocrator with four angels around him in a medallion in the middle of the dome; and there are images of the four Gospel writers on the pendentives. Also, there are pictures of saints on the tambour frame of the dome. There are eight richly framed pictures between five reciprocal windows illuminating the main floor from the northern and eastern directions.

The iconostasis including three naves at the eastern end, the ambon that sits on the cross rank at the south eastern end, and, in front of it, the despot throne situated between the cross ranks at the south eastern end of the main floor, are made of marble and ornamented with herbal and geometric motives of sculpture and relief technique.

36 YERRORTUTYUN (SURP) CHURCH

It is situated within the Fish Bazaar at Sahne Street, İstiklal Avenue in Beyoğlu district. It is also known as Church of the Three Altars. It is known that a building consisting of four floors, situated on the site of the present church, was used as a place of prayer for ten years after 1503. A school was constructed here in the 19th century, which was converted to a church by permission of the Sultan, and took the name of "Amenasurp Yerrortutyum" in 1807. The church was ruined after the fire of 1810. Permission needed for the construction of the new church

wasn't given until 1835. Construction of the church, commenced under the direction of the architect of Hassa, Garabet Balyan, Hovhannes Serveryan and Hamamcıbaşı (Keeper of the Royal Bath) Minas Agha in 1836, was completed in 1838 and put into religious service. Related additional buildings were constructed around the church in 1846. The epigraph, prepared for the 100th anniversary of the church's construction in 1907, was put above the window on the main façade of the church. The church and wooden structures that were damaged in the fire of

1870 were reconstructed. The church was restored in 1890. The last major restoration to the church was carried out in 1989.

The church is spread out over a large area. One enters the church and the narthex by the main entrance on the western façade. The narthex has three sections. The lateral areas are three steps higher than the middle one. Three lines of columns appear between each of these sections. There is a gallery above the narthex. The middle area opens directly onto the main floor through a four-leafed iron door. This main floor is arranged in the shape of nine transverse modules. Wooden barriers separate the section after the seventh module from the place where prayer is performed. The subsequent section belongs to the spirituals and the choir. The throne of the bishopric is reserved for the use of the Patriarch. One passes through the northern door in this section to Surp Dzınunt Chapel, which is used as a Baptistery, and to Surp Krikor Lusaroviç Chapel by the southern door.

The apse is five steps higher than the main floor. One ascends to the apse through stairs at the southern and northern ends. There is an altar on each of the rectangular niches that appear on the wall at the east of the apse.

The doors located in the northeast and southeast of the apse open into small lateral rooms, the passages, and lateral chapels.

There is a tomb of the Patriarch Iknadios Kakmacıyan I of Istanbul at the exit of Surp Krikor Lusavoriç Chapel (1869). However, the tomb situated at the exit of Surp Dzınunt Chapel belongs to Çulfalı Hagopas IV. The marble altar, placed in the niche right in front of the marble basin of the baptistery in this chapel, is interesting.

The main floor of the church and the chapels are barrel-vaulted. The floor of the church's garden is paved with white marble. The wooden main altar is the most attractive element in terms of ornamentation in the church. The interior area was constructed in the style of Greek-Byzantine architecture. Corinth order was used in the interior area. However, the exterior facades were designed according to Doric order. Iron doors appearing on the exterior façade also include some ornamental elements.

37 SAINT ANTOINE CHURCH

It is located between Galatasaray and Tünel on Istiklal Street in Beyoğlu district. The church is situated in a court, which can be reached by passing through an arched door between the apartment houses on the street, which belong to the church. The church and the apartment houses are the works of the architect Giulio Mongeri (1875-1953), who was born in Istanbul. The original name of the church, which was under the direction of Italian priests, is San Antonio, but it is known as Saint Antoine. Construction of the church commenced in 1906 and it was put into religious service after its completion in 1912.

The church, constructed in an east-west orientation on land that slopes to the east, measures 25x50 meters, and is a Latin cross planned structure. The width of the structure extends to 30 meters with columns that protrude at the transept. The interior height reaches 23 meters in the middle nave. The height at the eastern façade of the church reaches 56 meters due to the slope of the land. The apse makes a polygonal projection with five facades on the outside. The belfry appears above the southern apse next to this projection. The western façade, which contains the main entrance of the church, forms a

rectangular projection in the direction of the middle nave. This projection has three sections. There are three entrance doors opening from the middle section to the main floor of the church, and from the lateral sections to the lateral naves. The outer façade of the church is faced with brick.

The main floor has three naves and there are two rows of six columns each between the naves. The middle nave and the transept were kept higher than the lateral naves. The roofing system is completed with cross-ribbed vaults, which is another emphasis of gothic architectural style. The three apses bounded by the transept at the eastern end are

St. Antuan in the Miniature Museum of Miniaturk İstanbul

four steps higher than the main floor. There is a door connecting to the belfry and the monastery at the southern end of the transept. The organ appears in the lodge above the main entrance at the west. The wood-carved statue of the Crucifixion hung on the altar, and the gold-gilded wooden statue of Saint Antoine, are the works of Italian sculptor Luigi Bresciani. Also, there is a bronze statue of Pope John XXIII in the court of the church.

There is a two-floor monastery building at the south of the church. The basement of the monastery is arranged as a church and its use was given to the Keldanis. One ascends to this place by stairs from the northern court. Two six-floor apartment buildings, connected to each other by a passage above the entrance of the court, were constructed in order to provide income for the church

38 SANTA MARIA DRAPERIS CHURCH

It is located between Galatasaray and Tünel on İstiklal Street in Beyoğlu quarter. The history of the church dates back to the 16th century. After the Church of Santa Maria, first constructed on Mumhane Street in Galata in 1584, was burnt, it was rebuilt on a plot of vacant land donated by Madame Clara Bratola Draperis of the Fransciscan cult, and "Draperis" was added to the name of the church because of this donation. The church, which was burned in 1660 and restored, was burned again in 1678.

After the church, which was constructed in Beyoğlu in 1691, was burned again in a fire, it was built of stone on its current site. Italian architect Guglielmo Semprini constructed the current building in 1904 in place of the building that was damaged in the great fire of 1870 in Beyoğlu. The picture of "The Virgin Mary" that survived the fire of 1678 is situated above the main altar of the present church.

The present church stands on steeply sloping ground in a manner that composes a complex, connecting the front most building with the Santa Maria Hostelry, which fronts onto Istiklal Street and has shops in its basement, and the public housings of the church on both sides. The hostelry was constructed at the same time as the church in order to produce revenue for the church.

One reaches the church by descending the stairs in the basement of Santa Maria Hostelry. There is an image of the Virgin Mary on a golden coloured background above the entrance door, which is in the middle of a simple and symmetric frontal façade in the neoclassical style of the church. The cross-vaulted narthex of the church leads through three doors to the main floor, which is built to a rectangular plan and is covered by barrel vault. The barrel vault over the main floor is ornamented with angels and different motifs. There are pictures of religious context on the walls. The apse is separated from the section belonging to the congregation by a flat parapet. The altar appears in the middle of the apse.

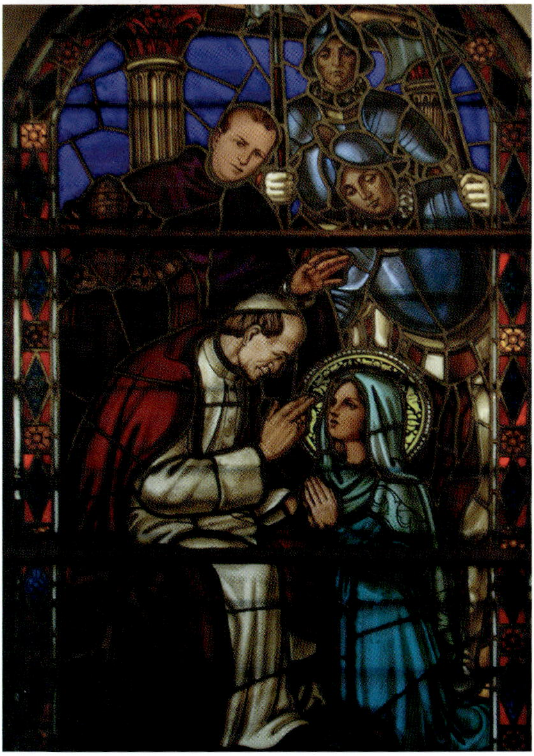

39 SAINT PIERRE and PAUL CHURCH

It is situated at Galata Tower Street in Beyoğlu district. It is also known as San Pietro and San Paolo church. The church, constructed between the years of 1841 and 1843 by Dominicans is a masterpiece of the famous Swiss architect Gaspare Fossati of Italian stock, who performed the great restoration of Hagia Sophia during the time of Abdülmecit. The church is located within an area of 20 thousand square meters along with its additional buildings.

The Dominicans came to Istanbul in 1228 and constructed a monastery next to San Paolo Church in Galata. When this monastery was converted to a mosque under the name of the Arab Mosque, they moved to San Pietro Church in 1475. This church suffered badly from the fire of 1660. Hereupon, the dining hall on the land of the church was converted to a church. After this structure was ruined in the fire of 1731, a wooden church building was constructed in 1732. However, in 1841, this old wooden structure was pulled down and the current church building constructed in its place.

This land, which slopes towards the Golden Horn, was split along the middle into two different levels by a sustaining wall in a north-south orientation. The church building at the lower level of the western section, with no street façades, is located parallel to the slope in a northeast direction, thus forming a court between itself and the sustaining wall. One enters, by a two-leafed door with an epigraph opening onto Galata Tower Street, into this long rectangular shaped court, which is connected to the monastery garden at the upper level by stairs at the east. The church has three naves, measures 35x8 meters, and has a height of 14 meters. An apse, protruding in a semi-rounded circle

along its width, bounds the structure. Its dais part is kept large. There is a big altar in the middle of the apse. Other than this altar there are also four small altars. The section where the priest celebrates the sacred ceremony is covered by a dome with a diameter of 8 meters, which has a blue background with yellow stars on it. The figures of four Dominican Popes are illustrated on the pendentives that support the dome. There are two doors in the square-planned narthex, one of which opens to the eastern court and the other passes through the building and opens onto the street. The third, frequently used, door of the church opens to the eastern court from the main floor. A vault that sits on the body walls and surrounds the entire place covers the single-naved main floor. A simple dome that sits on the pendentives covers the dais and a semi dome covers the apse. There is a barrel roof external to the vault and a ribbed roof on the dome. There are two balconies above the entrance door of the church's interior. Italian students were watching the sacred ceremony in these years from the second balcony. Neo-classical and empire styles dominate the structure. The organ made by Camillo Bianchi (1875) appears in the first balcony. The old monastery building at the western side of the church was constructed in 1837. The new monastery building, built between the years of 1928 and 1930, appears on the upper level of the site.

40 CRIMEA (ANGLICAN) CHURCH

It is situated in Serdarıekrem Street, which intersects Galip Dede Street in Beyoğlu. It is also known as the Anglican Church. The land, on which there was previously a Greek cemetery, was given to the English by Sultan Abdülmecit (1839-1861) for the construction of a church to commemorate the Crimean War (1853-1856). The architect of the church was G.E. Street. The construction of the church commenced in 1858 but, due to various interruptions, didn't finish until 1868 when the church was put into religious service.

The church was constructed in neo gothic style and its entire stone material was brought from the island of Malta. One enters the rectangular planned church from a western direction through an arched door. The main floor is barrel-vaulted

and the rectangular shaped apse is cross-vaulted. There is a platform with an elevation of one step in front of the main floor. Five steps lead from this platform to the area in front of the apse, separated from the main floor by barriers. This area, which was kept deep, was allocated to the spirituals and the choir. There are illustrations of saints and priestesses. The altar appears in the middle of the apse.

There is marble baptistery pool in the arched section protruding from the left wall of the church. One ascends to the belfry in the northeast corner of the church through the door next to the ambon at the right hand side. A small belfry appears in each of the northern and southern corners of the western façade of the church.

Because of the severely reduced size of the congregation, the church was closed for worship in 1970s. Under the leadership of the priest Ian Sherwood of the British Consulate, Sri Lankan Anglican refugees, who took refuge in Istanbul in 1991, restored the church and it was re-opened for worship.

41 KRIKOR LUSAVORIÇ (SURP) CHURCH

The church, located in Sakızcılar Street in Karaköy quarter in Beyoğlu district is the oldest Armenian Church in Istanbul. Although its exact construction date is not known, several historians accept it to be 1431. Two epigraphed stones in the church, one bearing an image of Calvary and the other with an image of the Virgin Mary and Jesus, carry the date of 1431 on them.

The mortal remains of Patriarch Krikor of Kayseri were buried under one of the walls of the church in 1635. Antoine Galland writes, in his travel book of 1672-1673, that the church of Surp Krikor Lusaroviç consisted of three sections. The church suffered badly in the fire of Galata in 1731. The church was opened again for worship after restoration. The church was largely damaged again in the fire of 1771. Surp Haç and Surp Garabet churches were completely burnt except for the church in the centre. After a wait of 28 years, the church was restored in a short time in 1799 by the architect Minas Kalfa, and opened again for worship in the same year. The church underwent a change of shape in 1888. Three churches, the centre formed by Surp Haç and Surp Garabet, are linked to each other, the walls between them being removed. During widening works on Kemeraltı Street in 1958, the whole church collapsed. The church was reconstructed to a plan prepared by the architect Bedros Zobyan and was opened for worship in 1965.

The current church was planned in an east-west orientation and its entrance is from the west. One enters the narthex of the church by passing through the feet of the two-floor belfry, which was constructed on four feet adjacent to the western entrance. The gallery is above the narthex. One descends stairs at the southern and northern ends of the narthex to Surp Amenapırgıç cha-

pel in the basement. The main floor comes after the narthex. A cylindrical-framed dome with sixteen borders covers the main floor. The elevation of the dome from the ground is 23 meters.

The section allocated to the choir and the spirituals is separated from the main floor, at its east end, by wooden barriers, on a one-step elevation. One ascends from this section to the dais section, at an elevation of 1.05 meters, by stairs of four steps at each of the southern and northern ends. The front of the dais is completely covered with old marble crucifixes. The main apse with semi-rounded dome appears in the centre of this dais. The altar is in the middle of the apse.

There are two small chapels with arched doors after the dais, on both sides of the apse. The southern chapel was dedicated to Surp Isadepanos, and the northern chapel is used as a baptistery. There are six niche units along the perimeter of the apse. The basement of the church was dedicated to Surp Amenopırgıç. Beneath the belfry was separated for the tomb of Hovhannes Golod of Bitlis. One traverses to the altar section after two columns in the front of the main floor. The central altar was dedicated to Surp Amenapırgıç and two others to Surp Tateos and Surp Partoğomenos respectively.

There are large pictures of the Priest Saint Mesrop Maşdotz, inventor of the Armenian alphabet, and of the Principal Patriarch Saint Sahag Bartev, in two ends of the dais section in the church. There are also four pictures in the narthex. The biggest of these is an image of the Virgin Mary carrying Jesus in her arms. Above the chapel doors on each side of the altar, the scene of the Crucifixion of Jesus is illustrated on one, and the scene of the "Resurrection" on the other. Also, Kütahya ceramics were used on the walls of the baptistery chapel, Surp Amenapırgıç chapel in the basement, and the tomb of Patriarch Hovhannes Golod.

42 CHURCH OF PANAYIA EVANGELISTRIA

The church, situated in the middle of a court surrounded by high walls between the streets of Kasap Hurşit, Hacı Ilbey and Mirimiran in Dolapdere in Beyoğlu district was constructed in an east-west orientation. The holy spring of Panayia Teotokos is at the north west end of the church and administrative buildings belonging to the church are at its south west end.

It is known that there was previously a wooden church here. The existing church, constructed in place of this church, was put into service in 1894, after work which took 16 years. The church was constructed from face stone with two colours. There are belfries of baldachin type at the north west and south west corners adjacent to the church.

The church is built to a rectangular plan and was constructed as a closed Greek cross. The church building consists of the main floor, a three-sided apse jutting out to the east, and the rectangular-planned narthex in a north south orientation. The entrance of the narthex is at the western end. The narthex has a flat ceiling and there is a gallery with two floors. These galleries are supported by two marble columns. One ascends to the galleries via stairs under the belfries, passing through the northern and southern ends of the narthex.

The main floor has a square plan and is covered by a central dome, supported by four columns. The columns are connected to each other by arches. There is an image of Jesus Pantocrator in the middle of the dome, and illustrations of angels on the pendentives. Also, there are various pictures of saints on the walls of the church. The wings of the cross-planned church are vaulted and there are single small domes at each

of the four corners of the church. There are three low-arched entrances to the main floor at the northern, southern, and western ends. The interior of the apse is covered by a round dome. The altar is in the middle of the apse. The rooms at both sides of the apse are used by priests as changing rooms. There is a marble iconostasis at the western end of the main floor. The marble ambon that sits on the north western column and the despot throne in front of the south eastern column are ornamented with herbal and geometrical motifs. The church was badly damaged during the events of September 6th-7th, 1955.

CHURCHES of the BOSPHORUS KADIKÖY-ISLANDS

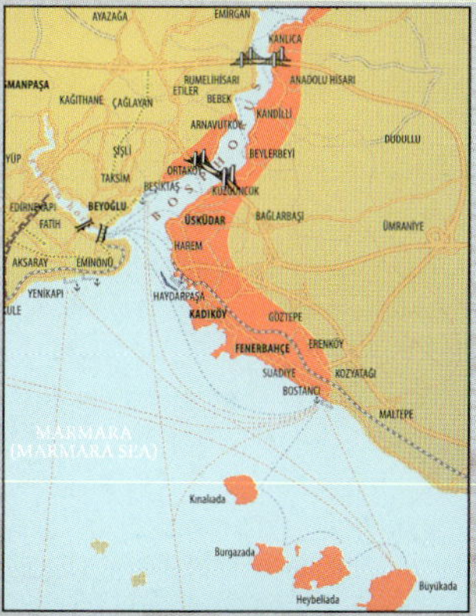

43 ASDVADZADZIN (SURP) CHURCH

It is situated in İlhan Street in Beşiktaş district. The church was possibly constructed in 1661 or between the years of 1681-1684. It was reconstructed on behalf of the Virgin Mary in 1838 with the support of Garabed Amira Balyan (1800-1866), the Palace Architect, in place of the church that was pulled down. The church has two domes. The belfry was added later on. The church was built in an east-west orientation on a cross-like plan with two gallery floors at the western end. First one enters the narthex. The left and right hand side sections of the narthex are three steps higher than the middle area. Four columns that appear in the narthex seem to be supporters. The narthex is separated from the main floor by an iron-framed fence. The four wings of the nave have vaults, which sit on the columns in the corners. All of the columns in the church are adjacent to the walls. The eastern wing of the nave is separated for the spirituals and the readers. Each side of this section leads to a small single-room chapel. These small-roomed chapels are covered by cross vaults. The northern chapel was allocated to the Baptistery, the southern one to the dressing of the spirituals and the readers. One climbs five large steps to the apse, built to a semi rounded plan. The church bell was installed in a cavity in the triangular pediment on the frontal façade of the church. The architect Garabad Amira Balyan made the first of the architectural ornamenta-

tions in the church during construction. The church underwent major restoration in 1987.

The vaults covering the four columns of the church, which is built to a cross-like plan, are ornamented with herbal motifs. There is an oil painting of Jesus in the centre of the dome. The letters, "HS" (Hisus/Jesus), "KS" (Krisdos/Masih), "DR" (Der/Lord) and "AZ"(Asdvadz/God) appear in ornamented garlands and rays at the ends the four arms of the cross.

Although the exterior appearance of the church is simple, its inside is extremely ornamented. The altar, gilded with gold leaf and situated on four columns in the middle of the apse, is a work of art in its own right. The large pictures of saints in the church are the work of Umed Beyzad, the Palace Painter.

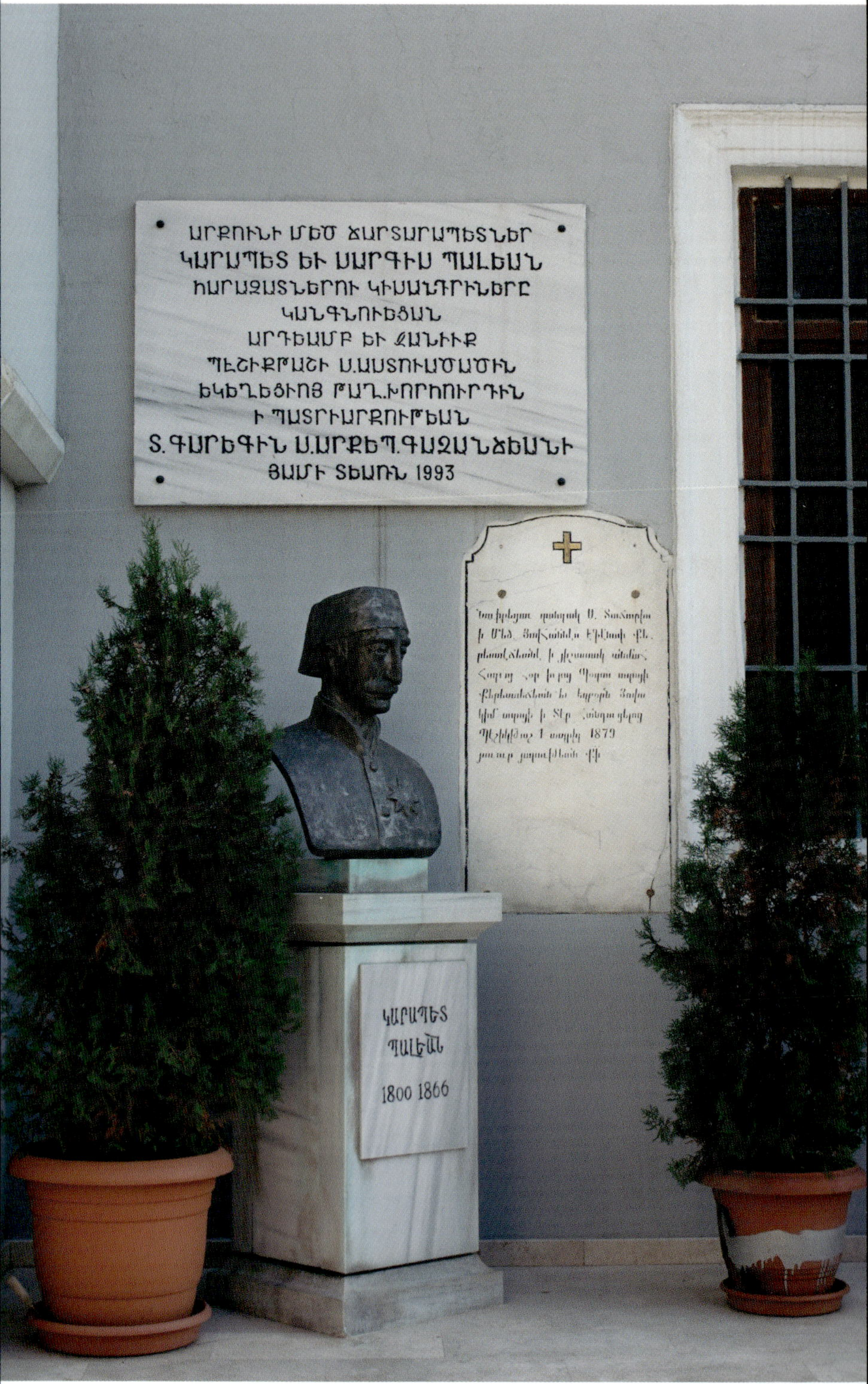
ԱՐՔՈՒՆԻ ՄԵԾ ՃԱՐՏԱՐԱՊԵՏՆԵՐ
ԿԱՐԱՊԵՏ ԵՒ ՍԱՐԳԻՍ ՊԱԼԵԱՆ
ՀԱՐԱՋԱՏՆԵՐՈՒ ԿԻՍԱՆԴՐԻՆԵՐԸ
ԿԱՆԳՆՈՒԵՑԱՆ
ԱՐԴԵԱՄԲ ԵՒ ՋԱՆԻՒՔ
ՊԷՇԻՔԹԱՇԻ Ս.ԱՍՏՈՒԱԾԱԾԻՆ
ԵԿԵՂԵՑՒՈՑ ԹԱՂ.ԽՈՐՀՈՒՐԴԻՆ
Ի ՊԱՏՐԻԱՐՔՈՒԹԵԱՆ
Տ.ԳԱՐԵԳԻՆ Ս.ԱՐՔԵՊ.ԳԱԶԱՆՃԵԱՆԻ
ՑԱՄԻ ՏԵԱՌՆ 1993
ԿԱՐԱՊԵՏ
ՊԱԼԵԱՆ
1800 1866

44 FOKAS (AYIA) CHURCH

The church is located on Muallim (Teacher) Naci Street in Ortaköy quarter in Beşiktaş district. Above the door of the church that opens to the street, there is a belfry with iron components. The church, constructed in 1856 is covered with a double faced ribbed roof on the outside. Access to the prayer area is via doors at the southern and northern ends.

The church, of masonry structure, is of a basilical plan type, and its

main floor has three naves. There are six lines of columns between the naves. The apse protrudes and is semi rounded in line with the middle nave. The altar is in the centre of the apse. The main floor and the naves are covered with barrel vault. There is a gallery on the west side of the main floor. The wooden iconostasis, the despot throne, and the ambon, are gilded with gold and ornamented in relief technique.

45 SURP HAÇ ARMENIAN CHURCH

It is situated at Kırbaç Street in Kuruçeşme and is an Armenian Gregorian church. There is a Greek Orthodox Church named Hagios Dimitros above this church. The church is located in a high court surrounded by walls. Besides the church there is also an unused Armenian School in the court, as well as some other buildings. The patriarch Zachary II opened the church for worship on February 28th, 1798 and the church gradually collapsed over the course of time. It was restored by Architect Garabet Balyan and opened for worship again on November 16th, 1834 by Patriarch Isdepannos Zakaryan II. After the wooden belfry and the walls were burned in a fire in 1919, an iron belfry was constructed later on.

The church was restored again in 1977 and 1988, bringing it to its current condition. Even today the church is still closed for restoration works. The façade of the church is very simple. The main church has a basilical and a cross plan. It was constructed in an east-west orientation. The narthex has a flat ceiling and the gallery is above it. The narthex opens to the main floor through an iron-fenced door. The main floor is separated from the section allocated to the spirituals and the choir by wooden fences. Doors at the north and south of this section lead to the chapels at the sides. There are small altars in each of the apses of these chapels.

The main floor is cov-

ԵՒ ԱՅԱ ԵՐԵՒԵՑԱՒ ՆՇԱՆ
ՄԱՐԴՈՅ ՅԵՐԿԻՆՍ

ered by barrel vault. One ascends to the apse by four steps on both sides. There are cells on each side of the semi-domed apse. The northern cell is the baptistery room and the southern cell is the treasury where sacred documents are kept. A gorgeous wood altar, overlaid with gold, appears in the middle of the apse. Pictures of saints belonging to old times appear on this altar.

46 DIMITRIOS (AYIOS) CHURCH

It is a Greek Orthodox Church located on Kırbaç Street in Kuruçeşme. The church was constructed on sloping ground in a basilical plan. There was another previous church in the same location during the Byzantine period.

The narthex of the church, which was constructed in 1798, is covered by a flat ceiling and opens to the main floor through three doors in the direction of the naves. There is a gallery above the narthex. The main floor has three naves. Three symmetrical apses protrude; one of them in the centre, two others at the sides. The apses are semi-domed on the inside. The main apse in the centre is bigger than the other ones. There are five lines of columns between the naves. The main floor and the lateral naves are covered with barrel vaults.

An illustration of Jesus Pantocrator appears in the middle of the vault covering the main floor. The ambon sits on the third column from the front of the northern column line. The despot throne appears in front of the second column from the front of the southern column line. The ambon and the despot throne were made using relief technique and were ornamented with herbal motives. The richly decorated iconostasis includes three naves at the east of the main floor.

The higher structure of the holy spring is accessed through a door opening from the northern nave. One can reach the main source, approximately 25 meters away from the structure of the holy spring, through a tunnel.

47 TAKSIARHES CHURCH

It is a Greek orthodox church situated on Satış Square between Dere and Abdullah Molla Streets in Arnavutköy quarter in Beşiktaş district. The church is in the centre of a court, surrounded by high walls. The holy spring of Ayia Paraskevi is at the south end of the church.

The church, constructed from hewn stone in the second half of the 19th century was built according to a closed Greek cross plan. There is a dome with a carved frame on the axes of double-faced ribbed roofs that cover the structure in east-west and south-north directions. Round arches connect four supporters, bounding the main floor, to each other. The arms of the cross and the places in the corners, along with the gallery, are covered by cross vaults. The illustrations of Jesus Pantocrator in the middle of the main dome and four bible writers on the pendentives are carved.

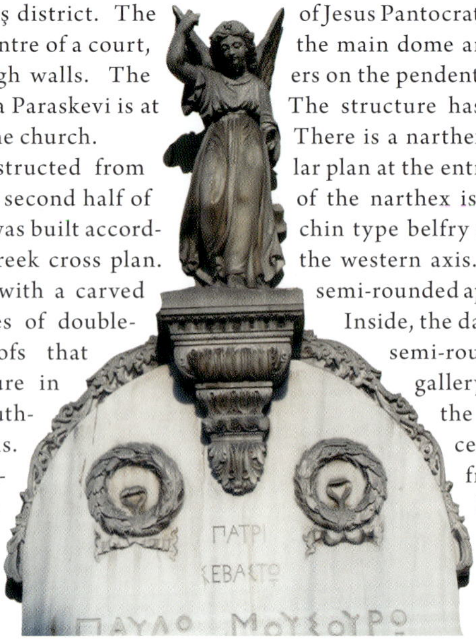

The structure has three entrances. There is a narthex with a rectangular plan at the entrance. The ceiling of the narthex is flat. The baldachin type belfry sits on the roof in the western axis. The protruding, semi-rounded apse is semi-domed. Inside, the dais is in front of the semi-rounded apse and the gallery appears above the narthex. One ascends to the gallery from the main floor by stairs at the north and south ends.

The iconostasis

situated at the east of the main floor is made of wood and ornamented with geometrical and herbal motifs. Again the ambon, located next to the supporter in the northwest of the main floor, and the despot throne, situated next to the supporter at the southeast end, are made in relief technique and ornamented with herbal motifs. There are images of the Virgin Mary and child Jesus in the gallery.

ΔΕΥΤΕ ΠΡΟϹ ΜΕ

48 NIGOĞAYOS (SURP) CHURCH

The church situated on Mehmet Yavuz Street in Beykoz district is set in a court surrounded by high walls. The church, first constructed in 1776, suffered badly in the earthquake of 1834, and was restored in a short time. The church fell to ruin due to lack of care over the course of time, but was restored in 1946 and opened for worship again. Finally the church was restored in 1962, 1974 and 1982.

The rectangular-planned church was constructed in an east-west orientation. There is a belfry of wooden construction, built as an annex to the church, in the southwest corner. One enters by the main gate to the narthex section of the church. The rectangular-planned narthex is built in a north south orientation and its ceiling is flat. The narthex consists of three sections and the lateral sections are higher than the middle section. There is a gallery above the narthex.

Access to the main floor is by an iron-fenced door. The main floor is bounded by the area allocated to the spirituals and the choir, which protrudes eastwards, and the semi-rounded apse is covered by a semi dome. The main floor is covered by barrel vault. There are two small rooms at the north and south ends of the section belonging to the choir and the spirituals. The room situated in the north is used as the baptistery, the room in the south as a dressing room for the spirituals and the choir.

The apse is three steps higher than the ground. The altar is in the middle of the apse. The church is the only one among Armenian churches in Istanbul whose altar is inlaid with mother-of-pearl. The door at the right hand side of the apse opens to the treasury room, situated in the rear. The church has a double-faced framework roof on the outside.

49 EUFEMIA (AYIA) CHURCH

It is a Greek orthodox church dedicated to Ayia Eufemia. Ayia Eufemia was a rich woman from Kadiköy, and a famous saint/priestess of the Greek Orthodox Church. According to legend, she was continuously followed and wished killed, but neither fire burned her nor did lions want to eat her. Finally, she was killed in 303 by a blow to the head. The day of Ayia Eufemia's death is accepted as a feast day.

During the Byzantine period the Ayios Basis Monastery was on this location. Later on, this place was used as the Ayia Eufemia Metropolite Monastery. Metropolite Zaharias II of Kadiköy enlarged the church in 1830. The church couldn't be protected well over the course of time but was renewed with the support of Metropolite Iokem III in 1993 and re-opened for worship.

The church is situated in a court, surrounded on the northern and eastern sides by the buildings at the corner

where Muvakkithane Street and Yasa Street intersect, within the bazaar of Kadıköy. The church, situated in an east-west orientation, was constructed according to Greek cross plan. Access to the narthex is by two doors that open to the court. There are silver coated icons and pictures on the walls of the narthex, and there are inscriptions embedded in the wall.

50 TAKAVOR (SURP) CHURCH

It is situated on Muvakkithane Street in Kadıköy. According to sources, it is known that there was a church here in the 18th century. The church, which began to deteriorate over time, was constructed again in 1814. It has been referred to as Surp Takavor Church because there is a chapel of Surp Takavor inside. The church, having suffered a lot in the fire of 1855, was reconstructed in 1858 and subsequently took the name of Surp Takavor Church. The architect of the church was Mıgırdiç Kalfa.

The church is built to a cross-like plan sitting on circles, in a departure from the usual basilical type architecture. One enters the narthex, which has a showcase, from beneath the wooden belfry at the western end. There is a gallery belonging to the choir. The narthex consists of three sections. The central section is rectangular and the lateral sections are of circular plan. One enters the main floor from each of the three sections of the church. At the eastern end of the main floor, the place allocated to the readers and the clergymen is separated by barriers from the main floor. There is a small chapel at the south of this section. However, a bigger chapel is situated at the northern end, dedicated to Surp Takavor. Here, there is a small church with a distinctive altar.

One ascends to the apse of the church by four steps at each of the northern and southern ends. The apse is built to a semi rounded plan and there is an altar in its centre. Gold leaf art also draws attention to the altar, which was built using wood engraving technique. The main floor of the church is covered with a dome whose tambour frame has round windows. The dome is coated with lead on the outside. The roof of the belfry resembles gothic architectural style.

51 KRIKOR LUSAVORIÇ (SURP) CHURCH

This church situated at Kınalıada is the only Gregorian church in Adalar district. In the 19th century, the Armenians living in Kınalıada applied to the Palace for the construction of a church on the island, in order to meet their worship requirements. Upon the firman dated 1854 of Sultan Abdülmecit (1839-1861) the foundation of the church was laid in 1855 on Livadya Street. The church, whose construction was completed in 1857, was opened for worship by Patriarch Hagop.

The church was constructed in an east-west orientation; one enters the rectangular planned narthex, built in a north-south orientation, from the west. The gallery given to the choir is above the narthex. The single-naved apse of the church is semi rounded and semi domed internally and protrudes outwards. The church is covered by barrel vault. One ascends to the apse by three steps on each side. The main altar is in the middle of the apse. On both sides of this main altar there is one small altar. The door opening to the north from the area belonging to the spirituals and the choir, in front of the apse, goes to the baptistery room, and the door opening to the south goes to the dressing room of the cantors. One reaches the gallery from the section next to the stone belfry, situated at the south western end of the narthex. The building, restored several times, was recently restored in 1988. Two pictures dated 1859 by the painter Ananyan of Hasköy are at the entrance of the church, a picture dated 1852 portraying the Crucifixion of Jesus, inside the church, and the image of the Virgin Mary dated 1830, decorate the walls. There are also some pictures of saints and of Mesrob Maşdots, the inventor of the Armenian alphabet on the walls.

52 LEVON (SURP) CATHOLIC CHURCH

The church, situated in a court surrounded by walls at Altıyol in Kadıköy district, was constructed in an east-west orientation, and is the only Catholic Armenian Church constructed on the Anatolian side. It is known that there was previously a wood chapel in place of this church. Permission to construct a masonry church in its place was obtained by firman of Sultan Abdülmecit (1876-1909) in 1905 and the church, whose construction was completed in 1911, opened to prayer.

The church, built to a rectangular plan, was built in Roman basilica style. The church measures 28.25x10.88 meters and has an elevation of 15.75 m. Still open for worship, the church was constructed by Imperial architect Boğos Bey Makasdar.

One enters the narthex through a door at the western end. The narthex, in line with the middle nave, opens directly onto the main floor. Above the narthex there is a "U" shaped gallery supported by square columns, which extends above the lateral naves. One ascends to the gallery up wooden stairs at the western ends of the naves.

Lines of three square-formed columns supporting the gallery continue as far as the middle section of the main floor. It gives the impression of a basilica with three naves. The ceiling as far as the line of columns at the eastern end is flat. The central main floor is barrel-vaulted while the ceiling of the dais and the apse are vaulted. The dais section was kept deep; however, the semi rounded apse section protrudes. The Patriarch throne appears at the northern side of the choir section. There is a sumptuous, marble decorated altar in the middle of the apse. There is one small altar each at both sides of the apse.

The choir section is a step higher than the main floor and is separated by wooden fences. One ascends three steps from

the choir section, not only to the apse, but also to the area where the patriarch throne stands. There is a belfry in the northeast corner of the church. The door in the southeast corner of the main floor opens to the dressing room; one ascends from the door at the northeast to the belfry.

Two doors open to the main floor from the narthex. One enters the main floor by descending three steps from the narthex. The main floor has three naves. There are four lines of columns between each of the naves. A dome with a high hoop covers the main floor. The apse is three steps higher than the main floor. The apse protrudes and is barrel-vaulted on the inside. The altar is in the middle of the apse. The iconostasis is at the east end of the main floor. The gallery, situated above the narthexes and the naves, is covered by cross vaults. The ambon appears at the left hand side of the apse while the despot throne appears in front of the dais at the right hand side. The belfry, constructed in stone is in the southwest corner of the church.

53 JOHN (AYIOS) PRODROMOS CHURCH (THE CHURCH OF JOHN THE BAPTIST)

It is situated on Göksemir Passageway Street in Burgaz Island. The history of the church dates back to the 9th century. It is known that there was a chapel built of wood there in those times. It is understood from literature that a stone church was constructed later on here and the current church was constructed in 1896. The church suffered badly in the earthquake of 1999 and was closed. It was re-opened on June 14th, 2007 as a result of restoration works that were carried out.

The church is oriented in an east-west direction and it was constructed according to basilical plan with three naves and a dome. There are belfries, one in each of the northern and southern corners of the west side of the church. The church has a square entrance with a flat ceiling. Access to the main floor is by a door with two wings. The main floor has a dome supported by four ranks. The dais section, which is one step higher than the main floor was kept deep while the apse section, covered by a semi rounded dome protrudes. The wings of the cross are covered by marble vault and there are small domes, one in each of the four corners. The main dome is externally coated with lead while other parts of the roof are tiled. There is an image of Jesus Pantocrator in the middle of the dome that covers the main floor, angels one each on the pendentives of the dome, the Virgin Mary and Child Jesus on the dome of the apse, two reciprocal angel images on the front side of the dais vault. There is an altar in the middle of the apse. The rich-looking iconostasis is in front of the dais.

There are rooms, one in each of the northern and southern corners of the east end of the main floor. One reaches the apse section from the northern room. The southern room was set up as a small chapel dedicated to the Priestess Paraskevi. The ambon sitting on the north western rank, and the patriarch throne situated in front of the south eastern rank, are made of wood and include decorations. Red tile was used as a decorative element on the window arches on the exterior facades of the church, and on the columns. One descends from the door at the left hand side of the entrance of the church to the cellar. During the Iconoclastic period, it is said that clergyman Methodios was imprisoned in this cellar by order of the Byzantine emperor. After the Iconoclastic period Methodios was elected Patriarch.

54 YEORYIOS (AYIOS) -GARIP MONASTERY AND CHURCH

The history of Ayios Yeoryios Monastery and Church, situated between Paradise Road and the seashore, lying down parallel with the shore towards the north of Burgaz Island, dates back to the 17th century. The monastery, which was constructed on the seashore is a long structure built to a rectangular plan. The monastery, with seven sections, also has seven different doors. It was renewed through restoration in different periods. White Russians, who left Russia and came to Istanbul after the Soviet / Bolshevik revolution, were installed in this monastery between the years 1919 and 1920. But the church was badly damaged by fire while the white Russians were living here and it was restored again.

Ayios Yeoryios Church stands between the monastery and the Paradise Road. It is known that the first church was on the seashore and was constructed in 1728. This church was pulled down in 1882 and reconstructed. During a strong earthquake which struck Istanbul this church collapsed completely. Hereupon, the current church was built in its present location in 1897. This church, largely damaged by the earthquake of 1999, was restored in 2004 and opened for worship in 2005. The bell, in three different sizes, on a tripod in the court of the church, is famous. Furthermore, there is also a tomb in the shape of an obelisk whose owner is not known. The holy spring of Ayios Nikolaos, protector of sailors, is at the lower part of the church.

The church, constructed in an east-west orientation has a closed Greek cross plan. There is a narthex with a flat ceiling. Images of religious content appear on the walls of the narthex. One traverses from the narthex to the main floor through a door. The main floor

of the church has a dome with a high tambour frame sitting on four supporters. There is an image of Jesus Pantocrator in the middle of the dome, and illustrations of the gospel writers on the pendentives. The other wings of the church are covered with barrel vault. Four corners of the church have a small dome each. The iconostasis appears in front of the apse. The despot throne is at the right hand side of the main floor. The apse juts out and its interior roof is barrel-vaulted. The altar is in the middle of the apse. The walls of the main floor are ornamented with pictures of religious content. The main dome of the church is coated with lead on the outside and other parts of it are covered with tiles.

55 NIKOLAOS (AYIOS) CHURCH

This church, in Heybeliada, situated on the corner where Ayyıldız Street and İşgüzar Street intersect, was dedicated to "Ayios Nikolaos", who is the protector of fishermen and sailors according to Christian belief. It is known that there has been a church here since the Byzantine period. After the old church was burnt down, a new wooden church was constructed here in 1790. But this church was also burnt down in 1856. At this time, the prohibition on building domed churches was lifted. Therefore, Ayios Nikolaos Church, built to very large dimensions, was constructed here with a dome. The architect of the church was Hadji Stefani Gaytanaki Kalfa. The bell of this glorious structure was brought from Tsarist Russia. There is a marble epigraph above the interior main entrance of the narthex of the church.

The domed church, constructed according to a basilical plan, has three naves. The dimensions of the church were kept considerably large; its length is 23.32 meters, its width is 15.33 meters, and its height is 8.66 meters. The church has a large narthex. Access to the main floor is through three doors from the flat-ceilinged narthex. The low-framed dome that covers the main floor sits on four columns. There are small windows all around the hoop. The lateral naves, the dais and the apse are covered with barrel vault. The altar is in the middle of the protruding apse. Besides the main dome, there are small domes, one in each of the four corners of the church. There is an image of Jesus Pantocrator on a medallion in the centre of the main dome. Illustrations of the gospel writers appear on the pendentives of the dome. The marble iconostasis, situated at the eastern end, the despot throne in front of the southeast column, and the ambon sitting on the northwest column, exhibit good examples of rich wood workmanship.

The icon of the Virgin Mary named

"Panayia Mirtidiotissa" and the icon named "Ayia Varvara" dated 1895 by Stavro Zografos of Heybeliada, and the icon called "Ayios Trifonos" dated 1909 by Apostolos Zagrafos are important works of art which appear in the church. Ayios Nikolaos Church is used for worship, especially during the summer by Armenians and Syrians who don't have churches in Heybeliada.

56 YEORYIOS (AYIOS) CHURCH

It shares its name with Ayios Yeoryios Monastery, and is located on Yüce Tepe (202 meters), the highest hill in Büyükada. The monastery buildings were constructed around a court in 963 by Nikephoros Phokas III (963-969), along with the churches of five regions (churches of Ayios Apostoli, Ayios Haralambos ve Ayios Vlaherna / Blachernae). Today, there is an empty church belonging to the monastery. There is also the holy spring of Ayios Yeryios. The monastery was completely destroyed during the Latin invasion (1204-1261). As the only remaining building of the monastery, construction of the church of Ayios Yoeryios commenced in 1905 and it opened for worship in 1909. There is a marble belfry of baldachin type above the entrance gate of the court.

One enters the church by the door opening to its northern nave from a square planned and barrel vaulted structure, appended to the northern end of the church. The church, constructed on an east-west axis, was built of hewn stone and to a rectangular plan with three naves. Its western door opens to the holy spring and the monastery. The lateral naves are separated from the middle nave by four lines of columns. Marble vaults connected the marble columns to each other. The whole interior area is covered by cross vaults and the apse is semi-domed. The altar is in the middle of the apse. The apse makes a projection with three external facades. The ambon sits on the second column from the front of the right column row and the wooden despot throne sits on the third column from the front of the left column row. There is an image of Jesus within a round frame at the centre of the cross vault that covers the main floor while images of the four gospel writers appear at the transverse. The iconostasis, including the three naves at the eastern end has precious icons. The most important one of them is the icon of Ayios Yeoryios, which

is silver coated. A dragon killed by Ayios Yeoryios is illustrated here. It is said that this icon was embedded in the ground to protect it from the Crusaders, and the sacred table was placed over it in order to preserve it from the rain. The original of this icon is at the Greek Patriarchate in Fener.

It is said that this icon is 1500 years old and was brought to the church of Ayios Yeoryios from the convent in Maden. Jesus and his twelve apostles were illustrated on the table and on the door that opens to the terrace; the relics of Agios Pandaleimon- Ayia Eugenia and some other saints can be found amongst other icons. In the night when May 5th turns to May 6th an unusual kind of visit takes place at Yeoryios (Ayios) Church. Starting from the Union Circus, people climb up a sloping thorny route, taking 25 minutes in order to reach Yeoryios (Ayios) Church and to pray throughout the night.

INDEX

BIBLIOGRAPHY

Arseven, C.E.	*Eski Galata ve Binaları, İstanbul, 1989*
Eyice, Semavi	*Son Devir Bizans Mimarisi, Türkiye Toring Otomobil Kurumu Yayınları, İstanbul 1980*
Eyice, Semavi	*Ayasofya I (1984) II (1984) III (1986) Yapı ve Kredi Bankası Yayınları, İstanbul*
Eyice, Semavi	*İstanbul'un Camiye Çevrilen Kiliseleri, TAÇ, S. 2 (1986)*
Gilles, P.	*The Antiquities of Constantinople London, 1729*
İncicyan, P.G.	*XVIII. Asırda İstanbul, Çev. H.D. Andreasyan İstanbul 1956*
Janin, R.	*"La Geographie Ecclessiastique de l'empire Byzantin" Les Eglises et les Monasteres, Cilt III Paris 1953*
Komisyon	*Geçmişten Günümüze Beyoğlu, Cilt I- II İstanbul Büyük Şehir Belediyesi Yayınları İstanbul 2004.* *a) Zafer Karaca, Rum Ortodoks Kiliseleri.* *b) Hıristomos Kalaycı, Rum Kiliseleri.* *c) Ermeni Kiliseleri.*
Karaca, Zafer	*İstanbul'da Osmanlı Dönemi Rum Kiliseleri, Yapı ve Kredi Bankası Yayınları, İstanbul 1995*
Kömürcüyan	*XVII. Asırda İstanbul, Çev. H.D.Andreasyan, İstanbul 1952*
Mango, Cryl	*Byzantine Architecture, New York, 1976*
Mathews, T.F.	*The Byzantine Churches of İstanbul, Pennsylvania 1976*
Müller-Wiener, W.	*Bildlexikon zur Topographie İstanbuls, Tübingen 1977*
Özbilge, A.F.	*Fener - Balat - Ayvansaray, Bağlam Yayınları İstanbul 2005*
Peschlow, Urs	*Die İrenenkirche in İstanbul, Tübingen 1977*
Salzenberg, W.	*Altchristliche Baudenkmale von Constantinopel Berlin 1854*
Tarih Vakfı	*İstanbul Ansiklopedisi Cilt : 1 - 8 , Tarih Vakfı Yayınları, İstanbul 1993*
Tuğlacı, Pars	*İstanbul Ermeni Kiliseleri, İstanbul 1991*
Türker, Orhan	*Fenari'den Fener'e / Bir Haliç Hikayesi, Sel Yayıncılık, İstanbul 2001*
Türker, Orhan	*Halki'den Heybeliye / Bir Ada Hikayesi, Sel Yayıncılık, İstanbul 2003*
Turnalı, Esin	*İstanbul Kiliseleri, Kenthaber İnternet sitesi, İstanbul*
Underwood, P.	*The Kariye Camii, Cilt I-IV, Washington-London 1968*
Üsdiken, Behzat	*Pera'dan Beyoğlu'na, Akbank Yayınları, İstanbul 1999*
Wülzinger, K.	*Byzantinische Baudenkmaler zu Konstantinopel, Hannover 1925*